We love ya!...
And where you go we'll follow...
'Cause we support the Sporting...

The 2013 season.
Match by match.
March to December.

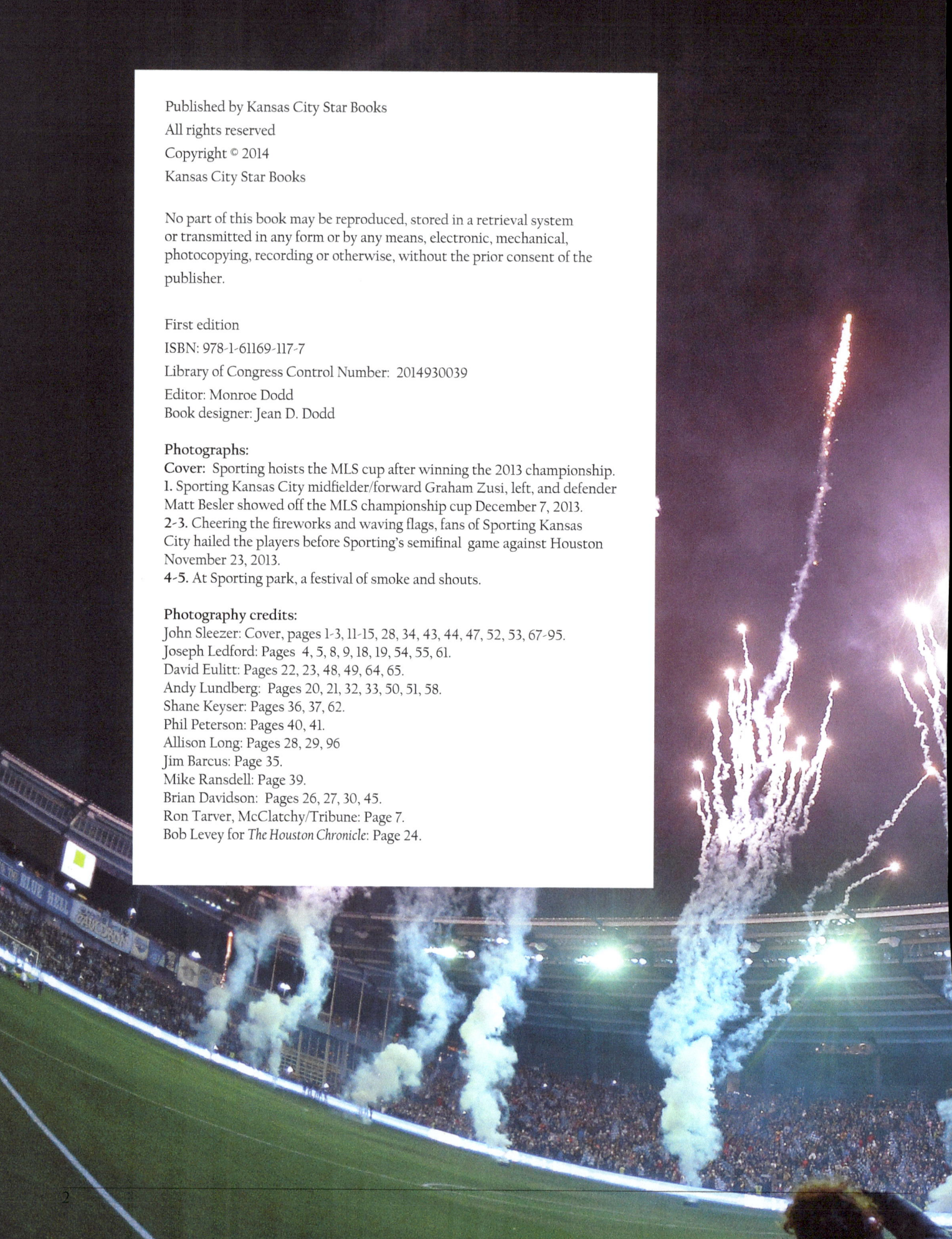

Published by Kansas City Star Books
All rights reserved
Copyright © 2014
Kansas City Star Books

No part of this book may be reproduced, stored in a retrieval system or transmitted in any form or by any means, electronic, mechanical, photocopying, recording or otherwise, without the prior consent of the publisher.

First edition
ISBN: 978-1-61169-117-7
Library of Congress Control Number: 2014930039
Editor: Monroe Dodd
Book designer: Jean D. Dodd

Photographs:
Cover: Sporting hoists the MLS cup after winning the 2013 championship.
1. Sporting Kansas City midfielder/forward Graham Zusi, left, and defender Matt Besler showed off the MLS championship cup December 7, 2013.
2-3. Cheering the fireworks and waving flags, fans of Sporting Kansas City hailed the players before Sporting's semifinal game against Houston November 23, 2013.
4-5. At Sporting park, a festival of smoke and shouts.

Photography credits:
John Sleezer: Cover, pages 1-3, 11-15, 28, 34, 43, 44, 47, 52, 53, 67-95.
Joseph Ledford: Pages 4, 5, 8, 9, 18, 19, 54, 55, 61.
David Eulitt: Pages 22, 23, 48, 49, 64, 65.
Andy Lundberg: Pages 20, 21, 32, 33, 50, 51, 58.
Shane Keyser: Pages 36, 37, 62.
Phil Peterson: Pages 40, 41.
Allison Long: Pages 28, 29, 96.
Jim Barcus: Page 35.
Mike Ransdell: Page 39.
Brian Davidson: Pages 26, 27, 30, 45.
Ron Tarver, McClatchy/Tribune: Page 7.
Bob Levey for *The Houston Chronicle*: Page 24.

SPORTING KANSAS CITY
WE LOVE YA!
2013 MLS CUP CHAMPIONS

By Tod Palmer, Sam McDowell
and the staff of The Kansas City Star
With a foreword by Sam Mellinger

KANSAS CITY STAR BOOKS
KANSAS CITY, MISSOURI

We love ya!

Foreword

The most Sporting Kansas City moment of all came an hour or so after the 20th penalty kick sailed high above Jimmy Nielsen's head and into the maniacs in the Cauldron. The moment was so quintessentially Sporting KC that it should be put on a plaque outside the stadium and printed on the team's business cards.

Already, this was the most important and powerful night of Sporting KC's re-branding, or even of the 15 years the club spent as a mostly forgotten franchise called the Wizards, or Wiz, in stadiums either much too big or entirely too small.

The field at Sporting Park was frozen. Fans warmed themselves with each other and constant motion and, for many of them, some beer, too. They stood and they screamed for a full 90 minutes, then 30 more in overtime, and then through two rounds of penalty kicks — by this time, each team could've won the MLS Cup a few times already.

Graham Zusi missed a kick — didn't even put it on goal — that would've won it at the end of the first round, and after that, you had to wonder whether maybe this wouldn't be Sporting's night.

But as they did throughout the playoffs — from behind three times against New England in the first round, once against Houston in the Eastern Conference finals, and again against Real Salt Lake in the championship match — Sporting's players kept their heads down and their hearts calm and made it work in the end.

The celebration included tears from Jimmy Nielsen and screams from Matt Besler and champagne poured onto the somewhat famous hair of Zusi. Sporting CEO Robb Heineman made for a particularly interesting reveler, a beer in his hand and black eye on his face after tripping over a dog gate at his home earlier in the day.

So, anyway, the celebration is at that point where the screams have settled and the guys are drinking their beers as much as they are spraying each other with them, when an MLS guy in a suit goes looking for the trophy.

Now, you have to understand, suits with the MLS are very stern about their Cup. Only specific league employees are allowed to touch it before the championship, and even then, only when they're wearing white gloves.

After the championship, there is a strict schedule for the trophy. The $100,000 piece of hardware crafted by Tiffany and Co. makes a TV appearance with the team, then gets passed around among the players. Once that all dies down, the trophy goes back to the green room for a scheduled photo session with league and soccer dignitaries ... and here comes The Sporting Moment:

Nobody knows where the heck the trophy went.

Turns out Heineman had kidnapped it and taken it to the Members' Club, where it started another happy riot. Of course that's where it was. Sporting has always made its own rules, and always centered those rules on its fans. Why would things be any different after a championship?

Anyway, by the time the league folks had figured out what had happened and taken the trophy back for their pictures, well, let's just say the thing was not in mint condition. (If you ever see one of those photos snapped that night with the league suits, look closely: You'll see fingerprints and scratches and maybe even a small dent or two. Sporting had to have the trophy polished three times in the first two weeks after the championship.)

After "Hotel California" stopped playing on the Sporting Park speakers that night and the stadium had been cleaned, there was one more quintessential Sporting moment still to come. Sporting KC technical director Peter Vermes mixed in some work with the celebration and didn't leave the stadium until 7:30 the next morning. Two days later, he was on an airplane to England to do some scouting.

There are more trophies to win and, at least momentarily, lose.

— *Sam Mellinger*

We love ya!

March 2
vs. Philadelphia Union
at PPL Park, Chester, Pennsylvania

W 3-1

The scoreboard must have lied. Anyone watching knew there was no way to explain Sporting Kansas City's victory over the Philadelphia Union in the Major League Soccer season opener.

Even Sporting coach Peter Vermes and his players knew it had to be faulty arithmetic, because for the first 35 minutes the visitors were getting so thoroughly whipped at both ends of the field they were fortunate to be down even a goal. Simply getting to the locker room tied was a feat all itself, setting the tone for a second half where they gradually took control, then pulled away.

But if not for the heroics of goalkeeper Jimmy Nielsen, it wouldn't have mattered. Nielsen surrendered one early goal to Sebastien Le Toux, but bailed his club after that until the rest came out of their funk. Once Graham Zusi hammered home the equalizer in the 41st minute — converting a fat rebound created by newcomer Benny Feilhaber's point-blank shot — the two-time reigning Eastern Conference regular-season champs were able to carry the momentum to the locker room, then emerge a different team in the second half.

"I think the first 35 minutes were a little unacceptable from our side," said Nielsen, who had a busy night. "We didn't play like men. We were all over the place. And they did a great job putting pressure on us. But in the second half we adjusted a bit and didn't allow them to counterattack."

Thanks to goals from 20-year-old Spanish import Oriol Rosell in the 66th minute, then Claudio Bieler's insurance tally 16 minutes later — with Zusi assisting on both — Sporting KC won its opener for the fourth straight season. Rosell is the youngest player in franchise history to play in a season-opening game.

"It's their home opener, so you expect them to come out and drive the game and put us under pressure," Vermes said. "They did a pretty good job of it.

"It was big for us to get that (tying) goal, so we didn't have be chasing the game the second half. What I liked is that we never panicked. We stuck with the game plan and just made a couple of adjustments."

> "...we never panicked. We stuck with the game plan and just made a couple of adjustments."
>
> — *Peter Vermes*

It didn't hurt that the Union, disheartened to let Sporting draw even by intermission after completely dominating the action, couldn't sustain the pressure. Ultimately it cost them when C.J. Sapong — fresh off the bench — drew a foul that resulted in a free kick. Zusi's ball was delivered perfectly to Rosell's head, putting the visitors ahead to stay.

And Nielsen made sure they remained in front, robbing Philly's Jack McInerney in the 79th minute before Bieler converted Chance Myers' pass, providing breathing room.

"Our mind-set changed after they scored a goal," said Feilhaber. "After that we were able to play our game, impose ourselves on the road.

They realized just how fortunate they were.

"This gives us confidence on the road that we can come back from being behind," said Zusi. "Statistics in this league are not very high for that. You don't

March

Sporting Kansas City's Aurelien Collin, left, and Philadelphia's Sebastien LeToux went up for a ball in the first half.

usually see road teams come back and win games when they give up a goal.

"That shows our character to be able to dig down and do that." And make it a smooth ride home.

Sporting league record: 1-0-0

9
at Toronto FC
Rogers Park,
Toronto, Canada
L 2-1

Two early gaffes by Sporting Kansas City helped Toronto FC to its first victory over Sporting in eight matches.

Claudio Bieler cut Toronto's lead to 2-1 with a little more than 10 minutes remaining, but Toronto's bunker-like defense held up late.

The 25,991 in attendance were brought back to their feet shortly after the national anthems ended when Toronto's Robert Earnshaw intercepted a lazy pass from the normally steady Matt Besler and buried a close-range shot past goalkeeper Jimmy Nielsen.

Referee Fotis Bazakos pointed to the penalty slot in the 21st minute when Paulo Nagamura hauled down Toronto's John Bostock. Earnshaw put Toronto's ensuing penalty past Nielsen, who dived the opposite way.

Coach Peter Vermes' decision to replace Bobby Convey with C.J. Sapong helped Sporting find its footing after the break. With Toronto in a defensive shell during the late stages, Sporting's sustained pressure finally paid off in the 77th minute, when Sapong flicked a long restart on to Bieler, whose first-time half-volley cut the lead in half.

Sporting league record: 1-1-0

March 16
vs. Chicago Fire
at Sporting Park

0-0

Chicago didn't seem to have much interest in playing soccer against Sporting KC and instead kept numbers behind the ball in a snooze-fest reminiscent of the inaugural game at the stadium two years ago.

We love ya!

In the last 14 years, Sporting Kansas City is 9-1-4 in its home opener. Three of those draws now have been of the scoreless variety against the Chicago Fire.

Winless in two games this season, Chicago didn't seem to have much interest in playing soccer against Sporting KC and instead kept numbers behind the ball in a snooze-fest reminiscent of the inaugural game at the stadium two years ago.

"It's a tactic, and I can't fault anybody for doing it," coach Peter Vermes said. "That's the way they play, but obviously that's not our style, but I think you're playing with fire — no pun intended."

Chicago, outscored 5-0 in the first two games, was content to sit back much of the night and let Sporting control possession. As a result, the stats were one-sided. Sporting held the ball 73 percent of the time and logged 608 passes — with an impressive 82 percent success rate. Chicago, on the other hand, made below 60 percent of only 221 passes.

"If they can defend for the full 90 minutes, that's great for them," midfielder Paulo Nagamura said. "We actually like it, because it gives us more time on the ball and more possession, which is how we want to play."

Sporting also suffered a league-high 20 fouls. The Fire racked up four yellow cards.

"I promised myself I would not complain too much about that, because it's one of the things we can't do much about," goalkeeper and captain Jimmy Nielsen said.

Sporting outshot the Fire 20-7, but put only three of those shots on goal. Chicago managed one shot on goal. In other words, there wasn't much for the crowd of 19,868 — the 17th straight sellout for Sporting KC — to get excited about.

"We still need that final ball," forward C.J. Sapong said. "We did well to keep it in their half, but every time we played the final ball it was either too hard or maybe we took a bad touch. The execution part in the final piece of the puzzle is what was missing."

Chances were few and far between.

Making his first MLS start in place of injured right back Chance Myers, defender Mechack Jerome tested Fire goalkeeper

Chicago Fire defender Austin Berry, left, kept the pressure on when Aurelien Collin, center, tried to head the ball in for a score.

Sean Johnson with a 25-foot roller in the 13th minute.

One minute after coming on for midfielder Benny Feilhaber in the 77th minute, forward Soony Saad ripped a 20-yard curling shot toward the near post from the left flank, missing the potential game-winner by a foot. In the 86th minute, with the Fire finally pressing a bit, hoping to steal a win off a fluke goal or careless play defensively, Sporting KC sprang forward on the counterattack. A nifty back-and-forth between Graham Zusi and Sapong led to a chance from 12 yards out by Zusi, but the shot sailed high.

"I'm disappointed in the fact that we didn't get three points," Vermes said. "There's nothing you can do when a team drops nine guys within a 24-yard space."

Sporting league record: 1-1-1

March 23

vs. New England Revolution

at Gillette Stadium, Foxboro, Massachusetts

0-0

We love ya!

Unlike the Chicago Fire last week, the New England Revolution didn't pack numbers behind the ball and waste 90 minutes against Sporting Kansas City. Still, the result was identical — a draw, thanks mostly to an uncooperative Mother Nature.

"The weather was horrible and it was a miserable environment to play a game in, but the guys did an excellent job to get out of here with a shutout and a point," coach Peter Vermes said.

Temperatures hovered in the upper 30s during the game, but sustained 20 mph winds made precision passing and any semblance of a buildup challenging, if not impossible.

"The wind was the No. 1 factor in the game," said midfielder Benny Feilhaber, who was traded from New England to Sporting KC in December. "The turf was a little bit tough too. Both teams ended up basically playing a field-position game — almost like it was football — putting it in one end, trying to press and seeing what comes of it."

Without its rock — midfielder Graham Zusi, who is playing with the U.S. men's national team — Sporting's attack never established any rhythm. The Revolution won more duels and owned a 55-45 edge in possession. Although Sporting outshot New England 13-3, most of those chances, including the game's only five shots on goal, were from distance and didn't trouble Revolution goalkeeper Matt Reis.

The good news is that Sporting's defense — which was without starting centerback Matt Besler, who also is on the U.S. men's World Cup qualifying roster, and starting right back Chance Myers, who has a nagging quad strain — didn't concede much of anything.

Ike Opara, who was acquired in an offseason trade with the San Jose Earthquakes, had a few shaky moments early, but put together a steady performance in his first start with Sporting KC. Meanwhile, Mechack Jerome, who was signed off Orlando City SC's roster a few days before the season, was rock-solid again as Myers' replacement.

"The guys did an excellent job not to give anything away," Vermes said.

Sporting KC nearly grabbed the lead in the 73rd minute when forward Claudio Bieler slipped behind the Revolution defense on a quickly taken, long restart similar to the sequence he scored on late at Toronto FC. Bieler tried to chip a shot over Reis' head, but the cagey New England veteran snuffed the opportunity.

"That was a great diagonal ball into space by Mechack," Vermes said. "I still say the commitment from the boys was fantastic in challenging circumstances."

Playing into a strong headwind in the first half, Sporting created the best goal-scoring chances, including a shot that pinged off the New England crossbar in the 19th minute.

It started with a long throw-in from Seth Sinovic. The ball pinballed around the box off center backs Aurelien Collin and Opara before settling at forward C.J. Sapong's right foot for a blast that took a deflection and clanged off the pipes. Feilhaber corralled the rebound, but he wasn't able to get much power behind a shot that Reis gobbled up with ease.

Sporting league record: 1-1-2

> **"The weather was horrible and it was a miserable environment to play a game in..."**
>
> *— Peter Vermes*

"All he needs is a little bit of space"

Claudio Bieler just wants to win.

Sporting Kansas City signed Bieler as the third Designated Player in club history on December 18, 2012, and the early returns were promising — a goal in each of his first two games. Of course, he came with a reputation as a prolific goal scorer.

Bieler, a native of Argentina, who turned 29 one day before the season opened, transferred to Sporting KC as the all-time scoring leader for LDU Quito, where he scored 57 goals in 110 appearances in Ecuador's Serie A. Overall, he had 71 goals in 155 appearances in his career.

"He's got an incredible finishing touch," says centerback Matt Besler, who is the reigning MLS defender of the year. "He's not the fastest guy and he's not the biggest, but he's shown the first two games that all he needs is a little bit of space."

In his MLS debut, Bieler iced a 3-1 win March 2 at the Philadelphia Union. He nearly sparked a comeback a week later when he scored in the 77th minute of a 2-1 loss at Toronto FC. But sitting at a mediocre team record doesn't sit well with Bieler.

"I'm not happy with my performance yet," Bieler said through Sporting videographer Abner Aceves, who served as translator. "I still have much more to prove. On a personal level, it's great to score a goal in the first two games, but the important thing is to win."

Some of the details get lost in translation, but he's

Claudio Bieler: A goal scored and aiming for more.

gone so far as to seek divine intervention. In his first season with LDU Quito in 2008, Bieler struck a deal promising a certain saint that he'd get the religious icon tattooed on his left forearm if the saint — known to grant an individual's wish, but at a price — would deliver a championship in the 2008 Copa Libertadores. After Bieler scored eight goals in helping LDU Quito become the first team from Ecuador to win South America's most prestigious club tournament, he lived up to his end of the bargain.

"I got it after we won as promised, but then things started going bad and I covered it up," Bieler said with a laugh.

Now, Bieler's left arm is covered with a sleeve tattoo depicting three Archangels — Gabriel, Michael and Uriel.

It's a faith he came by honestly growing up in Vera, an agricultural hub of roughly 50,000 in the northeast corner of Argentina's Santa Fe province and roughly 450 miles from the capital, Buenos Aires.

Sporting KC midfielder Graham Zusi said: "I'm not going to sit here and try and predict... but if he stays fit and continues to play the way he does, he's going to score goals."

A bounty of goals from Bieler probably means a bushel of wins for Sporting — and that would make everyone happy.

We love ya!

March 30 vs. Montreal Impact at Sporting Park

W 2-0

> "We had a very specific way we wanted to play the game and we executed it about perfect."
>
> — Peter Vermes

The Montreal Impact: perfect no more.

Sporting Kansas City, two-time reigning Eastern Conference champion, served notice that it wasn't prepared to give up that crown without a fight.

Behind an early goal from Claudio Bieler and a late goal from Graham Zusi, who recently returned from international duty with the U.S. men's national team, Sporting sent Montreal to its first loss of the season, 2-0.

"Outstanding performance today," goalkeeper Jimmy Nielsen said. "It was so attractive. It was so sexy to watch that I was so proud down there. That's the best soccer I've seen since I've been here and the best soccer we've played since I came here."

After playing back-to-back scoreless draws against defensive-minded opponents, Sporting welcomed an Impact side that was intent on going toe-to-toe with the Eastern Conference's top power broker.

Big mistake — much to the delight of the 18,609 in attendance, the club's 18th straight sellout.

Sporting KC jumped in front in the fifth minute when Montreal defensive midfielder Patrice Bernier, who has been terrific with three assists in Montreal's first four games, played a dreadful roller through the midfield. Bernier was trying to connect with a wide-open Hassoun Camara on the right flank, but Sporting defender Seth Sinovic intercepted the pass halfway to its destination and quickly passed ahead to midfielder Benny

In the fifth minute, Claudio Bieler scored past Montreal defender Matteo Ferrari....

Feilhaber. Feilhaber surveyed several options while continuing forward before picking out forward Claudio Bieler.

Bieler, brought in as a Designated Player to punch up Sporting KC's attack, lived up to his reputation as a clinical finisher with a gentle touch around Montreal centerback Matteo Ferrari and a crisp blast past Impact goalkeeper Troy Perkins at the far post.

"Claudio was wide open," Feilhaber said. "One thing I wanted to do this game was drive at the defense. When I picked up that ball, I had no other thing in my mind than to just go at them and see what opened up. Claudio made a great run off the centerback and it was an easy choice to give him the ball."

The fifth-minute goal was the second-fastest in Sporting Park history

... and received exuberant congratulations from teammates and the crowd. Benny Feilhaber, jumping, got the assist.

during an MLS match. Forward Kei Kamara, who is on loan at Norwich City, has the fastest — a fourth-minute goal last August against the New York Red Bulls.

Sporting KC dominated the first half, outshooting Montreal 10-1 in the first half.

"From the opening whistle to the final whistle, we were dominant," manager Peter Vermes said. "We had a very specific way we wanted to play the game and we executed it about perfect."

Montreal's first real goal-scoring threat came in the 60th minute when forward Marco Di Vaio tried a left-footed volley from the top of Sporting KC's penalty box, but Nielsen punched the ball to safety.

Sporting KC didn't relent in the second half, and broke through again in the 80th minute. Feilhaber corralled another loose pass by the Impact at midfield, and then threaded a ball forward through three defenders for Graham Zusi, who cut in front of Karl Ouimette, withstood contact and then chipped a shot behind a sliding Perkins. Impact coach Marco Schallibaum was ejected in the aftermath of going down 2-0.

Montreal actually had a slight edge in possession, but only managed one shot on goal and was outshot 21-6.

"The few times when they started to break the line a little bit, we made great recovery runs and our back line did a really good job of absorbing pressure," Vermes said. "Then, they really didn't have anywhere to play, because they were very narrow on the field."

Sporting league record: 2-1-2

April 5
vs. DC United
at Sporting Park
W 1-0

"It was a sloppy game, but at the end of the day we were able to get the result, and we're showing a lot of character the last couple games."

— C.J. Sapong

We love ya!

On the day U.S. Soccer celebrated its 100th birthday, Sporting Kansas City and D.C. United didn't treat fans to the most artfully rendered match of the last century.

Still, the home crowd of 18,988 – the club's 19th consecutive sellout — left happy after Designated Player Claudio Bieler's 89th-minute goal delivered a 1-0 victory.

"It was a sloppy game, but at the end of the day we were able to get the result, and we're showing a lot of character the last couple games," forward C.J. Sapong said.

The dramatic game-winner started with a turnover by D.C.'s defense deep in its own territory. Forward Soony Saad, who entered for midfielder Benny Feilhaber in the 83rd minute, stole a lazy back pass by Marcos Sanchez and then proceeded to nutmeg Marcelo Saragosa on the way to the end line. Once there, Saad slotted a ball back to the middle, where an onrushing Claudio Bieler drove a left-footed finish into the right side netting.

"We train that a lot in practice, cutting the ball back to the top of the box, so I stopped and the defenders kept going," Bieler said. "I was waiting for the ball and thankfully Soony put it there and I was able to finish."

It was the fourth goal in six games for Bieler.

"I've seen this finish here a million times in practice — not on me, on the other goalkeeper," goalkeeper Jimmy Nielsen joked. "But it's very important to have a solid goal-scorer, a guy who when he gets a chance sticks it in."

Before that, the third scoreless draw in the last four games seemed imminent for Sporting KC, which recorded its fourth consecutive shutout.

The game took on a sloppy tone from the opening whistle. Referee Armando Villareal issued five yellow cards in a turnover-filled, possession-devoid battle that featured only three shots on goal — two by Sporting and one for the United, which has yet to score in three road games this season. The game's first official shot came in the 18th minute when Matt Besler lobbed a throw-in into the box that Bieler headed a few feet wide of the right post.

Vermes: Rhythm was broken.

"(D.C.) had basically the back four with two in front and they really matched those guys up with our two attacking midfielders," coach Peter Vermes said. "I thought they did a good job tactically in regards to keeping it very compact and clogging the middle. It really broke the rhythm of the game."

Bieler and Feilhaber, a midfielder who arrived via trade with New England, worked a give-and-go in the United box during the 64th minute, but Feilhaber's blast sailed wide right.

With the shutout, Sporting KC extended its shutout streak to 429 minutes — the second-longest stretch in club history. During the 2000 MLS Cup championship season, Sporting KC didn't permit a goal for 681 minutes from April 19 through May 27.

Sporting league record: 3-1-2

C.J. Sapong, above, took a shot ahead of D.C. United defender Daniel Woolard. Left, Claudio Bieler began his celebration after scoring the game's only goal, leaping over a fallen Woolard.

We love ya!

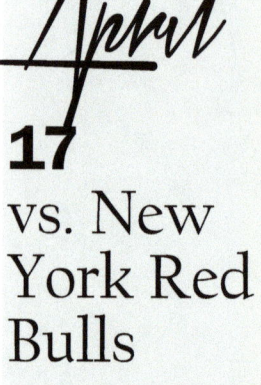

April 17
vs. New York Red Bulls
at Red Bull Arena, Harrison, New Jersey

W 1-0

Almost a year to the day after notching his last MLS goal, Sporting Kansas City defender Aurelien Collin headed home a Graham Zusi corner kick in the 13th minute. That was enough to secure a win for Sporting, which notched its fifth straight shutout and extended its shutout streak to 519 minutes.

"Before the game, we talked about how we saw some opportunities on set pieces," said coach Peter Vermes. "It was a great ball by Zeus, but it was also a great run by Collin with their guy all over him. For him to be able to get off the header with power, it was a great goal. Very good timing on the entire play."

Collin — who last scored during a 3-1 win April 18, 2012, at the Vancouver Whitecaps FC — muscled through Red Bulls centerback Jamison Olave and beat goalkeeper Luis Robles inside the right post. Left back Seth Sinovic ripped a shot from 20 yards out that Robles had to tip over the bar, setting up Sporting's third corner kick in the early going. And the third time was the charm as Zusi ripped a low, out-swinging corner that Collin met 10 yards from the near post before powering through Olave to get his head on the end of the pass. Collin now has seven career MLS goals.

The Red Bulls nearly knotted things up immediately. Juninho floated a 45-yard free kick toward Olave at the back post in the 16th minute, but goalkeeper Jimmy Nielsen came off his line and punched it away. Forward Thierry Henry corralled the rebound and took a rip at Nielsen, but the reigning MLS goalkeeper of the year was equal to the task again.

The Red Bulls' best chance to equalize came in the 64th minute, when defender Matt Besler misjudged a cross to the top of Sporting's box, allowing the ball to reach Henry for a free run into the box. Wary of an onrushing Nielsen, Henry tried to bury the ball inside the right post with the outside of his foot, but pushed the chance inches wide.

"When he gets those types of chances, he scores nine out of 10 times," Nielsen said. "Lucky for us today, that was the one he missed, because he's an absolutely outstanding player."

Ultimately, the Red Bulls joined a long list of teams unable to solve Sporting's defense.

"Last year, we were the best defense and this year we're still the best defense," Collin said. "It's a great reflection of the whole team.

"We gave up a couple chances tonight, but thank god they didn't score."

Sporting league record: 4-1-2

Kansas City argyles: "We thought it was cool"

Long rumored, the new uniform for Sporting Kansas City was rolled out in late April for the club's match against Portland.

The new alternate jersey featured a black top with an argyle pattern — using the club's primary colors, Sporting blue and dark indigo — across the front and black shorts. In the first four seasons of the franchise, 1996 through 1999, when it was known as Wiz and then the Wizards, the players wore black uniforms.

"We wanted to do something different," chief marketing officer Andy Tretiak said. "It's a special year because of Champions League and defending the U.S. Open Cup.

"The simple reason for doing argyle, though, is just

April 21
vs. LA Galaxy
at Home Depot Center, Carson, California

L 2-0

Sporting Kansas City's shutout streak ended at 545 minutes when the LA Galaxy also ended the visitors' five-match unbeaten streak with a 2-0 victory.

The game's fateful sequence started when Oriol Rosell slipped as he tried to gather a pass from Benny Feilhaber near midfield midway through the opening half. Rosell, who subbed off at halftime with a groin strain, recovered to challenge Galaxy midfielder Marcelo Sarvas for a 50-50 ball, but the Brazilian midfielder won the duel — though replays showed that Sarvas nudged the ball forward with a raised arm when the ball popped into the air.

With no whistle forthcoming, Sarvas played the ball wide for Landon Donovan, who had acres of space in the left channel. Donovan, who made his second start and third appearance since returning from a self-imposed hiatus, dribbled to the end line before beating Aurelien Collin with a series of chopping cutbacks and centering a pass to an unmarked Sarvas, whose left-footed tap made it 1-0 in the 27th minute.

"It was a terrible call by the referee, and obviously it changed the game," coach Peter Vermes said. "But that's the way it goes sometimes, and you've still got to be able to deal with the situation. But it was a 100 percent hand ball, for sure."

Sporting KC, which traveled 2,800 miles for the match after beating the Red Bulls in New York, faced only six shots on goal during its 545-minute shutout stretch, which was the fifth-longest streak in MLS history. Perhaps indicative of travel-weary legs, three of those shots on goal came in the opening 25 minutes against the Galaxy, which outshot Sporting 11-9 with five chances on target.

"We got out of shape a little too much," Vermes said. "I think some of that was because we were tired and we were getting to places late."

Donovan, whose 109 career assists rank fourth in league history, added his 125th career MLS goal in the 74th minute. He's third all-time in career goals. Forward Robbie Keane left Paulo Nagamura in his dust at midfield on a counterattack, drew Jimmy Nielsen off his line as he moved into the box and tapped the ball across the face of goal to Donovan for an uncontested finish.

Sporting record: 4-2-2

because we thought it was cool."

The logo of the club's jersey sponsor, Ivy Funds, runs underneath the patterned diamonds.

"It's something we fell in love with as we tried to create something practical for coming to the stadium to cheer at games, but also wearing away from the stadium as well," Tretiak said.

We love ya!

April 27
vs. Portland Timbers
at Sporting Park

L 3-2

Poor Chance Myers. Scoreless in 95 career games before this one, Myers broke through not once but twice, staking Sporting Kansas City to leads in the first and 29th minutes. Unfortunately for Myers and his teammates, neither lead stood up in a 3-2 loss witnessed by 20,186 — the club's 20th consecutive sellout.

"I got to enjoy it for about two minutes after each goal, but we didn't do enough to come away with the victory," Myers said. "There's no excuses. We've just got to be better. We got beat on a set-piece goal, which we usually don't do, and we got beat on a counter at home, which we usually don't do."

Myers put Sporting in front only 40 seconds into play, when he headed home a long-throw-in by Besler.

Ahead 1-0, Sporting coughed up the equalizer on a corner kick by Diego Valeri, who picked out Ryan Johnson in the middle of Sporting's penalty box. Johnson shed defender Matt Besler and redirected Valeri's low, out-swinging service into the upper left corner and over the head of a leaping Benny Feilhaber. It was the first goal Sporting had allowed off a corner kick since May 21, 2011 — a stretch of 75 games.

Myers put Sporting back in front in the 29th minute when Feilhaber lofted a cross into the box, which found Collin's feet for a square ball to the right post for an easy putaway.

Mere minutes later, Valeri triggered a 33rd-minute jailbreak when he played a ball into the left channel for Johnson, who sprinted past two Sporting defenders and into the box. Goalkeeper Jimmy Nielsen charged off his line, but Johnson coolly slid the ball across the face of the goal for Darlington Nagbe, who had two steps on left back Seth Sinovic and tied the game at 2-2 with a tap-in for his second goal of the season.

"The problem is we just gave the ball to the other team," coach Peter Vermes said. "You can't give balls away to the other team, so they can counter."

Portland scored the game-winner off another turnover-fueled counter in the 58th minute when forward C.J. Sapong and midfielder Paulo Nagamura couldn't connect on a short pass near the sideline. The misplay allowed midfielder Diego Chara to run at Sporting KC's goal with midfielder Uri Rosell trailing the play. Chara's diagonal ball found Rodney Wallace, who had squeezed between

> **"The problem is we just gave the ball to the other team."**
> — *Peter Vermes*

Matt Besler winced after being hit by Ben Zemanski of Portland.

Up in the air: Chance Myers, far right, headed a throw-in into the goal with only 40 seconds gone in the game.
Right: Seth Sinovic jumped to avoid being hit by Portland's Will Johnson.

Myers and Sporting KC's goal. He then rolled a shot under Nielsen, who allowed only three goals in the first seven games but has allowed five in the last two. The three goals allowed are the most since a 3-2 loss against FC Dallas on Aug. 27, 2011 — a span of 27 games.

Still, Sporting KC believes that — even with a few moments of sloppy play — three-goal games shouldn't happen, especially not at home.

"Obviously, we're losing the ball in bad spots, but it's also balance and spacing," left back Sinovic said. "If we're in the right spots when we lose the ball, we should be able to deal with it. Tonight, we weren't."

Sporting record: 4-3-2

May 5
vs. Chivas USA
at Sporting Park
W 4-0

What might have been: Claudio Bieler tapped in a rebound that would have given him his third goal of the game — except he was called offside.

We love ya!

Sporting Kansas City emphatically snapped its two-game losing skid by administering a beatdown of Chivas USA.

Forward Claudio Bieler notched his first brace, or two-goal game, midfielder Graham Zusi added a goal and an assist and forward C.J. Sapong ended a season-long scoring drought on a chilly afternoon with 18,811 in attendance. The event was Sporting's 21st consecutive sellout.

"The difference is every guy on the field worked from the opening minute to the final minute," coach Peter Vermes said. "The other piece is they all won their individual duels. When we do that here at home, we wind up dominating teams physically, technically, tactically and psychologically. Today, we broke that team."

Playing the final 33 minutes with a man advantage, Sporting didn't permit a shot on goal for the second time this season and eighth time in club history. It moved back into a tie for first place atop the Eastern Conference.

Things went sideways early for Chivas, which picked up the first of its four cards in the opening minute when defender Joaquin Velazquez took down Bieler a step outside the box.

However, it took until the 41st minute for the dam to break.

Making his first start since offseason shoulder surgery, Jacob Peterson's hustle to get to a loose ball forced Chivas USA right back Bobby Burling into a poor touch that Zusi pounced on before slotting it across the penalty area for Bieler. Bieler then chopped the ball around oncoming goalkeeper Dan Kennedy, who slid by. Kennedy was helpless to stop Bieler from cracking a left-footed shot between Burling and Carlos Borja for a 1-0 lead.

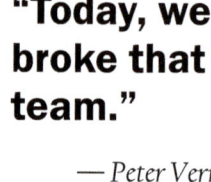

> **"Today, we broke that team."**
> — Peter Vermes

"I almost missed it," said Bieler, who didn't get much behind his shot, "but it's a reflection of my teammates. A lot of movement off the ball created a lot of problems for their defense."

It got worse — much worse — in the second half, when Kennedy was ejected in the 54th minute after taking down Paulo Nagamura at the top of the box.

Zusi, who was anchored in the middle of Chivas' half with his back to goal, played a direct ball for Nagamura off a quick turn. With the defense soundly beaten, Kennedy again came well off his line and wound up clipping Nagamura's right heel as he dribbled by toward an empty net. Referee Baldomero Toledo showed Kennedy a straight card for denying a goal-scoring opportunity.

Bieler, who now has an MLS-leading six goals in 10 games, made it 2-0 with a rocket into the left side on the ensuing penalty kick against Patrick McLain, who came in cold off the bench for Kennedy and guessed the wrong way.

Less than 10 minutes later, second-half sub Josh Gardner, who made his Sporting KC debut, set up Zusi for his third goal of the season with a cross from

20

Tangled up in blue and red: Jacob Peterson fought Carlos Borja of Chivas for control of the ball.

the left flank in the 65th minute.

Finally, Sapong, who came on for Zusi in the 67th minute, ended a season-long scoring drought in the 87th minute off a cross from Mechack Jeromes.

"It's been a while obviously," Sapong said. "I've been tested, but that's what makes it all the more beautiful when it goes in."

The four goals are the most Sporting KC has scored since a 4-2 win against Toronto FC on July 23, 2011, and tied for the most in Sporting Park history. Two of Sporting's two goals were waived off — one in each half — for offside infractions.

Meanwhile, goalkeeper Jimmy Nielsen recorded his MLS-best sixth shutout of the season and set a club record with his 38th shutout for the Wizards/Sporting KC.

Sporting league record: 5-3-2

Once again, the Seattle Sounders ripped out Sporting Kansas City's hearts in second-half stoppage time.

In a rivalry marked by fierce matches and late game-winners from coach Sigi Schmid's side, Seattle's Djimi Traore drove the latest dagger into Sporting KC's heart in the 95th minute.

Just when a scoreless draw appeared imminent, Zach Scott skipped a throw-in from the right side into Sporting's box, where Seattle's Brad Evans appeared to nick the ball in front of goal. Defender Aurelien Collin had a chance to clear the ball, but whiffed with a swing of his right leg. The ball wound up at Traore's feet. Catching a stunned Jimmy Nielsen flat-footed in the middle of the goal, Traore poked the ball into the right side and the Sounders escaped with a stunning 1-0 win.

"It was like jumping in an ice bath," Nielsen said of his reaction to the goal. "I was like, (geez) what's going on here?"

Seattle improved its record to 6-1-1 all-time against Sporting KC in MLS action. Seven of the club's 11 goals in the series have come in the final 15 minutes, including four game-winners in stoppage time.

In this game, it was an earlier giveaway by Collin that set in motion Sporting's undoing. In the 93rd minute, Collin was dribbling upfield uncontested after Nielsen collected a ball in the box and rolled it toward Collin, his All-Star centerback. But rather than blast the ball deep into Sounders territory, Collin tried a square ball to the left flank for Ike Opara, who was making his second straight start in place of an injured Matt Besler.

The pass — well wide of Opara — was intercepted by Seattle, which won the decisive throw-in a half-minute later.

"It is a monumental mistake as we came out of the back to play that ball square," coach Peter Vermes said. "At that point, we have Kei (Kamara) and C.J. (Sapong) up front, so that ball needs to be played forward. It's unacceptable to play that ball the way it was played."

The loss spoiled Kamara's return from a three-month loan with Norwich City of the English Premier League, where he notched a goal and an assist in 11 matches, including seven starts.

Sporting league record: 5-4-2

> **"It was like jumping in an ice bath."**
> — Jimmy Nielsen

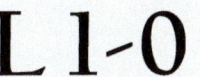

May 8
vs. Seattle Sounders FC
at Sporting Park
L 1-0

While Seattle midfielders Alex Casey, left, and Osvaoldo Alonso hugged in victory, Aurelien Collin hung his head.

Right: Kei Kamara headed the ball with Seattle defender Jhon Kennedy Hurtado. Alongside was Sporting's C.J. Sapong.

We love ya!

May 12

VS. Houston Dynamo

at BBVA Compass Stadium, Houston, Texas

W 1-0

Mechack Jerome cleared the ball from Houston midfielder Andrew Driver before Driver could advance on goal in the second half. (Bob Levey/For The Houston Chronicle)

Sporting Kansas City became the first visiting team in MLS history to win at Houston's new stadium, snapping the Dynamo's 36-match home unbeaten streak.

Exactly one year to the day after the $95 million stadium opened, Sporting posted its seventh shutout, 1-0, and rode a 73rd-minute goal by defender Aurelien Collin to the history-making win.

"We played the game tonight with a will and a fight," coach Peter Vermes said. "Those guys wouldn't be denied tonight. It's a great step forward for this group."

The Dynamo entered the match 17-0-7 at home in MLS games, including the playoffs, since BBVA Compass Stadium opened May 12, 2012. Houston also went unbeaten in the last 12 at Robertson Stadium.

Of course, Vermes and company also relished ending that run, especially in light of Houston's recent playoff success against Sporting KC.

The Dynamo ended Sporting KC's season in the 2011 Eastern Conference final and the 2012 Eastern Conference semifinals en route to back-to-back MLS Cup appearances.

The game's only goal came when Sinovic launched a ball into the middle of the penalty box with a Matt Besler-esque long throw-in. Collin found space amid a sea of orange-clad defenders and nodded a ball off his occipital bone past goalkeeper Tally Hall. Caught flat-footed at the near post, Hall had no chance to stop Collin's second goal of the season. Left back Corey Ashe valiantly tried to keep the ball out of the net with a diving head-first stab to no avail.

Asked whether he knew anyone who scored more goals with the back of his head than Collin, Sinovic said: "I don't think so, but it's pretty impressive. But it was really a great finish, because he had guys draped all over him."

> "We played the game tonight with a will and a fight. Those guys wouldn't be denied..."
>
> — Peter Vermes

The Dynamo didn't wilt, and instead ramped up the pressure in search of an equalizer, which almost came in the 80th minute. Midfielder Brad Davis drove a corner kick from the left side to the back post for rookie forward Jason Johnson, who was making his MLS debut. Johnson's header had Sporting goalkeeper Jimmy Nielsen beaten, but veteran midfielder Paulo Nagamura was in the right place at the right time to head the ball to safety.

Nielsen made a diving save on a header by Ricardo Clark two minutes later and also swallowed up a shot by Davis in the 88th minute to preserve the result as well as his MLS-best seventh shutout of the season.

"I can't make one critical comment about our team tonight," Vermes said. "The attention to detail, following the game plan and more importantly absolutely battling for every ball was fantastic."

The most significant development before halftime was the yellow cards referee Chris Penso issued to Collin and midfielder Oriol Rosell, the fifth of the season for both players who will be suspended for Sporting KC's next match at D.C. United.

Sporting league record: 6-4-2

May 19
vs. D.C. United 1-1
at RFK Stadium, Washington, D.C.

Sporting Kansas City settled for a 1-1 draw with Eastern Conference bottom-feeder D.C. United, but the result might have been dramatically different were it not for an offside call by assistant referee Matthew Nelson.

Defender Ike Opara appeared to stake Sporting to a lead in the 30th minute, but the goal was disallowed.

"There's no chance Ike was offside," coach Peter Vermes said. "The linesman doesn't understand the rule. Obviously, he made a big mistake."

The controversial play was set in motion when defender Matt Besler, who returned to the lineup after missing three games with a sprain, tracked down a ball at the end line. Besler cut the ball back to forward Jacob Peterson, who rolled the ball across the box where Opara blasted a right-footed one-timer into an empty net, only to throw his hands over his head in disbelief upon seeing Nelson's raised flag.

Replays showed that forward Claudio Bieler might have been offside at the opposite post, though even that was debatable. Bieler wasn't involved in the play, while Opara was more than a yard behind the United's last defender, Dejan Jakovic, in the middle of the goal box.

Sporting KC drew first blood in the 60th minute off a Graham Zusi corner kick. Opara nicked Zusi's service, which then clanged off D.C. defender Andrew White's noggin and into goal. D.C., which has only one win this season, equalized things in the 65th minute when Chris Pontius whipped a cross from the sideline toward the far right post, where Kyle Porter beat goalkeeper Jimmy Nielsen with a sliding shot.

Sporting league record: 6-4-3

We love ya!

May 26
vs. Houston Dynamo
at Sporting Park

1-1

Trailing by a goal at halftime, Sporting Kansas City salvaged a draw on forward Kei Kamara's first goal since returning to the club. Kamara, who has now played 116 minutes in four appearances, beat Houston goalkeeper Tally Hall with a left-footed roller inside the right post in the 68th minute.

"It was a tale of two halves," forward Jacob Peterson said. "First half, we weren't good enough. We didn't play with the sense of urgency that we needed to. I think we responded well in the second half. Because of the poor first half, we got the result we deserved."

> **"It was a tale of two halves."**
> — *Jacob Peterson*

One week after seeing a goal disallowed by a blown offside call in a 1-1 draw at D.C. United, Sporting KC was spared by a different assistant referee. In the 39th minute of the game, the referee took away a penalty kick for the Dynamo. Midfielder Brad Davis was making a run into Sporting KC's penalty box when Oriol Rosell slid in from the right side with a desperate challenge, tackling the ball away and simultaneously sending Davis sprawling.

Referee Drew Fischer, who moments earlier had whistled two quick fouls on Sporting roughly a minute apart, signaled for a penalty kick as coach Peter Vermes and the crowd of 20,876 — the club's 23rd

Jimmy Nielsen notched a save in the second half.

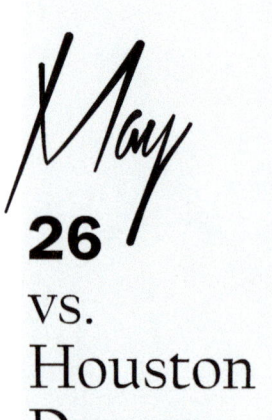

Brad Davis of Houston slide-tackled Kei Kamara.

May 28

vs. Des Moines Menace

Lamar Hunt U.S. Open Cup Third Round

at Sporting Park

W 2-0

consecutive sellout — erupted.

"It was no penalty kick," Vermes said. "Thank god that the other guys got involved. The assistant referee on the other side and I believe the fourth official got involved as well. They talked him off the ledge there."

After consulting with assistant Kevin Duliba the penalty was waived off.

Sporting's reprieve, however, didn't last long.

In the first minute of stoppage time, the Dynamo broke through when forward Giles Barnes flicked on a long restart from Houston's half, which Will Bruin collected before holding up play as Davis streaked into the box. Bruin made a quick turn and played the ball forward to Davis, who did the rest by slipping a ball between goalkeeper Jimmy Nielsen and the near post with the outside of his left foot for a 1-0 halftime lead.

Twenty-three minutes into the second half, Kamara evened things off a square ball from forward Claudio Bieler. Kamara, who moved alone into fifth place with 32 career goals for Sporting KC, took one touch left and then ripped a shot around a pair of Houston defenders, leaving Hall no time to react.

"It feels great, obviously, to score against your former team," Kamara said. Peterson, who nipped the ball to Bieler with a step-over move, was credited with a secondary assist on the equalizer.

Eight minutes after knotting the game, Kamara, who was traded from Houston to the then-Wizards in 2009, nearly put Sporting KC in front with a powerful header off an in-swinging restart by Zusi that Hall pushed inches over the crossbar.

Paulo Nagamura's sliding tackle against rookie Jason Johnson in the 94th minute snuffed out Houston's best chance to retake the lead.

Sporting league record: 6-4-4

Sporting Kansas City advanced rather easily in U.S. Open Cup play on goals from Kei Kamara and Claudio Bieler in front of an announced crowd of 15,621.

From the opening whistle, Sporting took control. In the 12th minute, midfielder Benny Feilhaber played a short corner to Mechack Jerome, who sent the ball on to Chance Myers in the box. Myers then rolled a rocket pass through the box, which Menace defender James Vollmer nicked with an outstretched right foot. That touch wasn't enough, however, to keep the ball from reaching Kamara, who hammered Sporting into the lead with a one-time strike.

Sporting eventually put the game away in the 73rd minute when Bieler redirected a cross into the goal for a 2-0 lead.

June 1

vs. Montreal Impact

at Sporting Park

L 2-1

While Sporting KC led at halftime, the Impact created the more dangerous chances.

C.J. Sapong got the ball away from Montreal defender Dennis Iapichino.

It was only early June, but Sporting Kansas City matched its season total for losses at home after a watching a halftime lead fade away.

Sporting took the lead in the fourth minute of first-half stoppage time when Claudio Bieler tucked a penalty kick into the lower left corner. Montreal vehemently protested the penalty and that anger seemed to carry over into the opening minutes after intermission. They proved decisive.

By the 53rd minute, the Impact had rallied into the lead despite coach Marco Schallibaum's being dismissed from the sideline for the second straight game at Sporting Park.

The second-half trouble started immediately for Sporting KC when right back Mechack Jerome picked up a yellow card near the end line for a reckless challenge against Felipe Martins. On the ensuing free kick, Montreal midfielder Sanna Nyassi drove a shot through traffic from atop the 18-yard box to knot the game in the 47th minute.

"We were not awake," said goalkeeper Jimmy Nielsen, "and we were not ready for them coming at us at that moment."

It got worse six minutes later. Sporting's defense struggled to clear a cross from forward Marco Di Vaio. The ball bounced around the penalty area and Peterson Joseph whiffed on a chance to clear it before the ball came to rest at Collen Warner's feet near the right post. With one swift strike, the Impact went in front on Warner's first career goal and Sporting's 1-0 halftime lead seemed a distant memory.

"You can't fan or whiff at the ball

Zusi: Not out of the blue

Graham Zusi, so the story goes, came from nowhere to become one of the best players in the U.S. and arguably the world. But that isn't entirely accurate.

"It's always discussed as a 'Where did he come from?' kind of thing,'" says his father, David Zusi. "But anybody who has followed Graham ... they all think it's more of a 'Finally, he's gotten what he deserves' type thing."

Graham, as unassuming and humble away from the field as his crosses into the penalty box are spectacular, thinks otherwise. For him, his rise is the product of hard work, a little luck and making the most of his opportunities.

"So much of success in sports is timing and being in the right place and having the right

mentor, all that kind of stuff," his father says.

From that perspective, Graham has been fortunate. His father was his youth coach for several years. Then came productive experiences under club and high school coaches in Florida before he headed for the University of Maryland and coach Sasho Cirovski.

"He was a tough guy, and he demanded things out of us," Graham said. "That's where I learned a lot of the discipline aspects of the game."

Now Graham has flourished under Sporting coach Peter Vermes and Sporting's technical staff.

Zusi's development on Vermes' watch is one of the main reasons he chose this year, at age 26, to re-sign with Sporting KC rather than chase dollars or prestige playing time in Europe. He will be under Sporting's control effectively through the 2017 season.

inside the box when it's played in there," said coach Peter Vermes. "You work too hard over the course of the game to give up two easy chances like we did."

The Impact controlled the first half and created the most dangerous chances.

"We've got to change our mentality and how we approach these games at home," Nielsen said. "When we got down 2-1, we went after them. But we should have gone after them from the first second of the game."

There was no mistaking the quality of Bieler's strike, but the sequence that led up to the penalty wasn't clear cut. First, defender Alessandro Nesta tugged on Bieler's jersey, but that infraction was outside the box. Then Nesta rested his right arm on Bieler's shoulder as a goal kick from Nielsen came bounding all the way down field. Bieler went down, referee Armando Villareal conferred with assistant referee Greg Barkey and the penalty was given.

With the win and the New York Red Bulls' loss, Montreal moved into first place in the Eastern Conference.

Sporting league record: 6-5-4

June 12

vs. Orlando City SC

U.S. Open Cup, fourth round at Sporting Park

L 1-0

Seth Sinovic saved the ball from going out of bounds in the first half of the match.

Orlando City SC, the most dominant team in USL Pro the last three seasons, struck less than 2 minutes into its match with Sporting Kansas City and the early goal held up for a 1-0 upset. Sporting, champion of the Lamar Hunt U.S. Open Cup in 2012, fell in the fourth found of this year's event to its own USL affiliate.

The Orlando goal less than 75 seconds after the opening whistle stunned the announced crowd of 15,981.

"It's devastating," coach Peter Vermes said. "The goal was a terrible mistake on our part."

Lions midfielder Adama Mbengue, who trained some with Sporting in the preseason, stepped in on a hastily taken restart deep in Orlando City's attacking end. Mbengue alertly booted the ball forward to unmarked striker Long Tan, who rolled a shot across goal to the left post — just ahead of sliding centerback Aurelien Collin's tackle and just out of the reach of goalkeeper Eric Kronberg.

Sporting, which knocked off the Lions 3-2 in the third round early in its march to the 2012 championship, controlled possession for much of the remaining 88 minutes, but finished with nothing to show for it.

The goal less than 75 seconds after the opening whistle stunned the announced crowd of 15,981

"We had a great opportunity at home and another unbelievable crowd, especially for an Open Cup game," left back Seth Sinovic said, "but we just couldn't get it done.

"We know what it feels like to win this thing and we all desperately wanted to do it again."

Sporting KC, which signed a two-year affiliate agreement with Orlando City of USL Pro in January

2013, outshot the Lions 18-5, including an 11-2 edge at halftime. Kronberg kept Sporting within striking distance when he stonewalled Tan in a one-on-one situation in the 33rd minute. Dashing to the top of the penalty area as the Lions' odd-man break developed, Kronberg smothered the ball as it came off the Lions striker's foot.

Meanwhile, Sinovic proved to be the most dangerous player for Sporting much of the time. He tried a shot from the top of the box, which halftime substitute C.J. Sapong redirected toward the left post in the 59th minute, but Miguel Gallardo preserved the shutout with a diving reflex save to his right.

Four minutes later, Sinovic debuted his David Beckham impression, bending a crisp 25-foot shot across the face of goal and toward the upper right corner, but it dipped a fraction of a second too late and went over the crossbar.

During the dying minutes, Ike Opara came within inches of tying the game with a slide at the far post, but — as was the case all night — that sorely needed goal wasn't meant to be.

Back at full strength at last, Sporting Kansas City was back on track, minutes away from an inspiring — and needed — road victory.

Then suddenly, shockingly, it all fell apart.

Sporting watched a comfortable two-goal lead evaporate into the hot Texas air when FC Dallas scored twice in two minutes to escape with an improbable draw. The result left Sporting disheartened, not to mention winless in MLS play in more than a month.

"It's deflating," defender Matt Besler said. "The disappointing thing is we put in 88 minutes of hard work and stuck to the game plan and did everything almost perfectly. And then three minutes later, we've given up two goals."

The turning point was a disputed red card shown to Sporting's C.J. Sapong in the 68th minute, which left Sporting down a man and gave hope to Dallas, leader of the Western Conference. The call came after Sapong and Dallas' Andrew Jacobson collided while contesting a header, and Jacobson fell to the ground in pain. As Jacobson was being attended to, a Dallas player kicked the ball toward the spot for the coming free kick. But the ball was headed straight for Jacobson and Sapong got his foot on it, trying, he said, to direct it away from the injured player. But the ball bumped Jacobson and referee Mark Geiger issued the card.

"It's funny, I was actually trying to stop the ball from hitting him," Sapong said. "The ref's back was toward me. I don't know if he thought I kicked him or I was sitting there and hit him with the ball.

"I thought it was very soft, if anything. I don't think we deserved a straight red.... For a straight red there has to be some kind of intent to injure or hurt a player, and my intent was completely opposite of that.... I don't want to say too much, but I'm obviously unhappy about it. It changed the game."

The difference turned out to be huge. Sporting KC was solidly in control. Sporting had scored on Kei Kamara's 43rd-minute penalty kick — set up when Jacobson was called for grabbing Aurelien Collin's jersey in the penalty area — and on an own goal in the 57th when Zusi's corner kick deflected off Dallas' Je-Vaughn Watson and into the net. Even after the red, Sporting's defense stood strong — until the 88th minute, when Jacobson gave his club life with a nifty backward header off a feed from Ramon Nunez.

With momentum and the home crowd suddenly solidly behind it, Dallas took advantage and struck again almost immediately. In the 90th minute, rookie defender Walker Zimmerman raced in from the left, beating Kamara to the front of the net and heading in David Ferreira's corner kick to even the score.

The tie left Sporting still looking for its first league win since stopping Houston's 36-match winning streak almost six weeks ago.

Sporting league record: 6-5-5

June

22

vs. FC Dallas

at FC Dallas Stadium, Frisco, Texas

2-2

Kei Kamara drove the ball past Columbus goalie Andy Gruenebaum for a goal.

June 29

vs.

Columbus Crew

at Sporting Park

W 3-2

Soccer matches don't get much wilder than Sporting Kansas City's victory over Columbus.

Forward Kei Kamara doubled his season total with goals in the 34th and 80th minutes, and Claudio Bieler added his team-leading eighth goal of the season.

"When we move off the ball like we did tonight, it's very difficult for teams to defend us," coach Peter Vermes said.

That's especially true when Kamara is active off the ball, as he was in fueling Sporting's first home victory in MLS play since May 5. The crowd totaled 20,128 — the 25th straight sellout.

"I tell him all the time, when he runs off the ball, I don't think there's a player in the league that's as dangerous or a player that can stop him," Vermes said of Kamara. "How are you going to stop a 6-3 guy coming at you who can absolutely fly down the field?"

Kamara's second tally delivered a late victory and obscured the fact, at least momentarily, that Sporting Park isn't the unbreachable fortress it once was.

For the second time this season, Sporting took the lead twice in the same game, but failed to hold either lead.

Sporting grabbed its first lead in the 34th minute when Aurelien Collin stepped up to pick off a misplayed ball from Jairo

Chance Myers and Tyson Wahl raced to catch a pass.

Arrieta and quickly tapped the ball to forward Soony Saad. From a few strides into Crew territory, Saad lofted a diagonal cross 40 yards from right to left. Kamara settled the skipping ball with a superb first touch and blasted Sporting into the lead.

Crew centerback Chad Marshall was unable to recover to challenge Kamara's shot, and Crew goalkeeper Andy Gruenebaum couldn't get off his line quickly enough to cut down the angle.

"I was just happy that Gruenebaum didn't get a touch on it, because he's a really good goalkeeper," Kamara said. "Anything that comes to him, he gets it."

Then came the first eight minutes of the second half.

Arrieta knotted the game at 1-1 in the 48th minute, sliding a shot under goalkeeper Jimmy Nielsen after a 65-yard run from the Crew's half of the field into Sporting KC's box. Two minutes later, Sporting retook the lead on Bieler's team-leading eighth goal of the season, which came courtesy of a Chance Myers cross — and after a slight deflection by Crew left back Tyson Wahl.

That lead didn't last either.

Three minutes after going back in front, Sporting allowed Columbus to knot the game again on an awful back pass from Seth Sinovic, who was tracking back on a ball and gently touched it back toward Nielsen. Trouble was, speedy Crew forward Dominic Oduro was in hot pursuit and beat Nielsen to the ball, tapping it around Sporting's befuddled goalkeeper and into an empty net.

"The two goals we gave up were just absolutely horrendous," Vermes said. "It wasn't good. It was terrible actually."

The match remained 2-2 until Kamara's goal in the 80th minute off a feed from Bieler. Kamara gathered in the pass and calmly drew Gruenebaum off his line before dribbling right and rifling the game-winner inside the near post.

Sporting league record: 7-5-5

> **"I tell him all the time, when he runs off the ball, I don't think there's a player in the league that's as dangerous."**
>
> — *Peter Vermes on Kei Kamara*

Jimmy Nielsen's journey to Kansas City

Sometime in early February 2010, Jimmy Nielsen's phone rang back in his native Denmark.

Nielsen, who is Sporting Kansas City's goalkeeper and captain, was miserable playing for Vejle Boldklub, which had been relegated from the Danish Superliga a few months earlier. With four years remaining on his contract and unwilling to play for the club anymore, Nielsen thought his professional soccer career was finished.

"I'd had enough with that club," Nielsen said. "If I didn't find anything else, I had two coaching offers — full-time — so I probably would have taken one of those."

Nielsen, who started the MLS All-Star Game in 2012 and went on to be selected as the league's goalkeeper of the year, wasn't ready to retire. He knew he had more good seasons in him.

Nonetheless, Nielsen thought he'd come to the end of the road.

"I wanted more," Nielsen says, "but the situation left me without many options. My club had all the power and control."

Then came that fateful phone call.

As a rule, Sporting coach and technical director Peter Vermes prefers to scout players in person. He made an exception for Nielsen.

"Normally, we try to go see a player live, but we didn't have that opportunity with Jimmy," Vermes said.

Vermes had caught wind that Nielsen wasn't

happy in Vejle. He'd seen "The White Puma" on film and was intrigued, but it was that phone call that cemented the deal.

"It was extremely motivating to talk to him on the phone," Nielsen says. "I had to put him on speaker, so my wife, (Jannie), could hear him, too. He basically told me about his plan for the team, a little bit about the city and organization and he got me — easily."

Vermes felt a similar instant connection.

"I could tell right away that he had a great attitude and he was a team-oriented guy," Vermes recalls. "It was strange. I could just sense it right away. I knew after talking to him that we'd get a deal done, and it was amazing. We got a deal in like 12 hours."

Usually, contracts in professional sports simply don't happen easily or quickly.

"It did in this case, because when we spoke, I trusted him 100 percent," Nielsen said. "He sent me an offer, and I accepted right away. It was pretty simple."

Only one thing stood in the way, Nielsen's contract with Vejle. That's when the gambler in him came out.

Back in 1999, Nielsen was playing for the Denmark under-21 national team when he and a couple of teammates sneaked away one night to gamble at a casino — in Vejle, interestingly enough. Once word of the escapade went public, Nielsen was banned from training with the national team and dubbed "Casino Jimmy," another moniker that has followed him throughout his career.

Nielsen doesn't gamble these days — Jannie barred him from Kansas City casinos — but he rolled the dice for a shot at playing with **Sporting** KC. He and Vermes had negotiated the framework of a one-year deal with an option for a second season, but Nielsen still had to persuade Vejle to let him go. That's when Nielsen bet big that he could rejuvenate his career in middle America.

"They wanted money from me, so I had to pay them some money myself to get out of the contract, and Kansas City paid a little bit, too," Nielsen said. "I'm just glad we figured out a deal."

It seems strange now, but Nielsen considered returning to Denmark after that first season in Kansas City.

"I spoke to a team back in Denmark and had it in my head for a few days," Nielsen said. Nielsen went 10-13-6 with 10 shutouts in 29 appearances for the then-Wizards, who were playing at CommunityAmerica Ballpark.

"I wanted to talk to Peter about it, but before that I talked to my wife. She said, 'Fine, you can go back to Denmark, but I guarantee you one thing, me and the kids are staying here.' That made that decision very easy and, of course, it was the right decision."

Nielsen posted seven shutouts and went 12-8-11 in 31 appearances in 2011, helping Sporting rally to win the Eastern Conference regular-season title. In 2012 he played every minute — an MLS record-tying 3,060 — and Sporting repeated as Eastern Conference regular-season champions. Nielsen went 18-7-9, matching the MLS record for wins in the non-shootout era and finishing with 15 shutouts, one shy of the league record.

"My plan was to come here for one year and get the motivation back and enjoy soccer a little bit, but now I enjoy life more than I ever have before," said Nielsen, now in his mid-30s. "It's a great organization. We have a great team here with a great future."

On the field or runway, Collin gets noticed

Aurelien Collin does everything with flair.

Of course, people don't often see past the Frenchman's rough-and-tumble playing style. In three seasons with Sporting Kansas City, Collin has developed a reputation as one of the toughest centerbacks in Major League Soccer.

"When we scouted him, we knew he was going to be good in our league," says coach Peter Vermes, who signed Collin in April 2011.

Collin's teammates have come to love his on-field style — a brash, hard-tackling blend that seldom fails to frustrate opposing strikers.

"Collin is our bulldog," goalkeeper Jimmy Nielsen says. "He's the fighter, and (central defense partner Matt) Besler is more of the elegant guy. Collin's doing the dirty work."

Away from the field, Collin, whose arms and back bear tattoos evoking angels and the cross, displays a similarly distinctive style. Each offseason he seems to post photos to Twitter from exotic beaches

Matt Besler in a Collin outfit.

on different continents every week. His thick French accent, easy smile and the ornery twinkle in his eye further burnish his playboy reputation.

Midway through the season, Collin showed his softer side with the debut of his new clothing line, AC78 — his initials and jersey number.

"I grew up in Paris and people really care about fashion there," Collin said. "People will talk to you in the street about what you're wearing."

"Fashion, my style on the field and my life are very connected," Collin said. "I want to design clothes for regular people with regular bodies and make the point that anybody can look great and look sharp in a suit."

The race so far

With the arrival of July came the midpoint of the season — 17 games played and 17 to go — and Sporting Kansas City was tied for third in the Eastern Conference standings.

With 26 points accumulated from a 7-5-5 record, Sporting sat three points behind the Montreal Impact, which had played two fewer games, and two points behind the New York Red Bulls, who had played one additional match.

So Sporting remained in the thick of a tense, tight race for the Eastern Conference championship as well as home-field advantage throughout the conference playoffs.

Western Conference frontrunner Real Salt Lake led the Supporters' Shield standings with 33 points from 18 games. FC Dallas and the Portland Timbers FC had 30 points through 17 games.

Consistency remained the buzzword for coach Peter Vermes.

"There are contributing factors and the guys coming in and going out is one," he says. "We're still trying to get some new guys that are here to adapt and adjust and acclimate to who we are."

"If we could win our division again, that would be fantastic," said goalkeeper Jimmy Nielsen, "but at the end of the day we've got to stand with the MLS Cup. I would take fifth in the division if that means finishing up with the MLS Cup. That's what we are playing for."

July

3

vs. Vancouver Whitecaps FC

at Sporting Park, Kansas City

1-1

Once again, Sporting Kansas City found itself sitting on a lead at home. Unfortunately, as was the too-familiar pattern in the season's first half, Sporting couldn't protect it. Instead, the team settled for a draw.

Sporting got on the board first in the 35th minute on a sequence set in motion by midfielder Oriol Rosell, who pushed up from his usual defensive midfield role with Paulo Nagamura sidelined by an ankle injury. It was Rosell's cross into the box toward the right post that right back Chance Myers pushed back toward the middle for Aurelien Collin.

Collin wheeled and tried to put a shot on frame with his left foot, but Vancouver defender Johnny Leveron blocked the shot. The deflection, however, fell to Collin's right foot for a swift blast past Whitecaps goalkeeper Brad Knighton. That sparked a raucous celebration from the crowd of 20,137, Sporting's 26th straight sellout in MLS competition.

Ahead 1-0, Sporting KC kept up its suffocating style — at least until the dying minutes before halftime.

With literally seconds left in the 45th minute, Camilo Da Silva Sanvezzo tied the game with a slick right-footed free kick from 25 yards out. Sanvezzo tucked the equalizer into the upper right corner over defender Matt Besler, who had been stationed at the right post, but ran off the line at the last second, and well out of goalkeeper Jimmy Nielsen's reach. It was Sanvezzo's 10th goal of the season, which is tied for the second most in MLS.

Before that, Sporting had the Whitecaps on their heels, keeping the game in Vancouver's half of the field and Knighton under constant pressure.

Sporting league record: 7-6-5

Left: Kei Kamara headed the ball as Vancouver defender Nigel Reo-Coker watched. Above: Kevin Ellis and Vancouver forward Corey Hertzog tried to win the ball out of the air in the first half.

We love ya!

July 7
vs. Chicago Fire
at Toyota Park, Bridgeview, Illinois

W 2-1

They couldn't have scripted a better start.

Sporting Kansas City scored two goals in the opening eight minutes, and those proved to be enough in a 2-1 victory that moved the club into a tie for first in the Eastern Conference.

"Any time you can win on the road, it's a big win and Chicago is a tough place to play," said defender Matt Besler. "We have to give credit to our fans, because they have traveled well the last couple years with 500 people or maybe more and we've gotten some good results. A lot of that is because of them and the atmosphere they create."

Sporting is only 4-15-2 all-time against the Fire in Chicago, but since 2008 the club is 3-2-1 at Toyota Park.

Making his first start since May 19, midfielder Benny Feilhaber staked Sporting KC to a lead in the sixth minute off a long throw-in by Besler. Besler launched the ball into the middle of the Fire penalty box, where forward Kei Kamara got a touch that sent it toward the top of the box. Feilhaber rushed in to collect the free ball and pinged a shot off the inside of the left post and past Chicago goalkeeper Paolo Tornaghi. Tornaghi was making his second straight start while regular Chicago goalie Sean Johnson prepped for the Gold Cup with the U.S. men's national team.

"A goal can do wonders for someone's confidence," mid-fielder Graham Zusi said. "I think (Feilhaber) will be even more dangerous moving on now."

Two minutes later, Feilhaber, Graham Zusi and Seth Sinovic harassed defender Jalil Anibaba into a turnover deep in Fire territory. The ball eventually came back to Zusi at the left edge of the Fire penalty box. Unpressured by Chicago's defense, Zusi lofted a cross toward the right post that sailed over Kamara's head, but it also sailed over Tornaghi's outstretched arm and into the side-netting for a 2-0 lead.

"It was a cross," Zusi admitted, "but we'll take it. I was a little surprised it went in, but happy nonetheless."

Yet the Fire wasn't exactly doused. Forward Chris Rolfe had two chances eight minutes apart — a rip from 25 yards away in the 10th minute that goalkeeper Jimmy Nielsen punched over the crossbar and a one-on-one chance in the 18th minute that Rolfe sent wide of the far post with Nielsen rushing out to meet him.

Eventually, Chicago broke through in the 38th minute, when Mike Magee timed his run perfectly to collect a pass from Jeff Larentowicz before sliding a ball inside the left post for his league-high 11th goal.

The second half didn't feature as much fluidity or as many chances — perhaps a product of both teams having played four days before along with muggy conditions and a lot of whistles.

Sporting had a golden opportunity to pad its lead in the 59th minute, but reigning MLS Rookie of the Year Austin Berry blocked shots by Kamara and midfielder Oriol Rosell in rapid succession to keep it a one-goal game.

Sporting has gone 2-0-1 during a stretch of three games in nine days, claiming seven of a possible nine points and beating two Eastern Conference foes — Columbus and Chicago — who were in hot pursuit in the standings.

Sporting league record: 8-5-6

For Ellis' family, sacrifice and a dream realized

There was a time Sporting Kansas City defender Kevin Ellis almost had to give up soccer.

As Kevin and his twin brother, Keith, got older and began playing for more elite club teams, the expenses mounted. Good coaching isn't cheap, and the Ellis boys were starting to rack up travel bills that strained the family budget.

"When we were kids, my parents didn't have a lot of money," Kevin Ellis said. "Eventually, it came down to either we both quit playing sports, because we couldn't afford it, or at least one of us did."

Soccer had become Kevin Ellis' life around age 3 when his late mother, Christina, enrolled her hyperactive toddler in a recreational soccer program. When her options began to dwindle, she didn't want to pull either son from soccer but had a talk with Keith.

"We were picking up Kevin from soccer practice, and I was in the car with my mom," Keith said. "She kind of told me the situation before he came to the car, and I basically just told her that Kevin loves soccer. I played more for fun anyway.

"I told my mom, 'Just Kevin can play. That's fine.' I was a little kid. I wasn't trying to do anything special."

"My whole family made sacrifices for me."

Look at him now: Kevin Ellis, a 2009 Oak Park High School graduate, is making history.

He became Sporting's first homegrown player to play in an MLS match when he subbed on for Seth Sinovic at left back in the 63rd minute on June 29 in a 3-2 win against Columbus at Sporting Park. Ellis then became the first Homegrown Player to start in a league match against the Vancouver Whitecaps.

"My mom ...made sacrifices for me," Kevin says.

Sporting's Kevin Ellis, exultant and appreciative.

"My whole family made sacrifices for me to be able to be here."

The brothers were close, as twins tend to be, but their mother's death strengthened that bond even more. It happened their sophomore year in high school.

"She had a cyst in her stomach, I think, that ruptured, so it was herniated," Keith said. "It was supposed to be a routine surgery, a 30-minute surgery, max. They messed something up, and she lost oxygen to her brain...and was in a coma for two months."

Christina lived three more years, until she was 47 — mostly in and out of hospitals with complications and congestive heart failure — but things were never the same.

"I think about my mom every day," Kevin said. "I told her everything. She told me everything."

Keith got choked up watching Kevin fulfill his lifelong dream.

"When you know someone's worked their whole life toward something, especially your twin brother," Kevin said, "it's crazy. He's my best friend and one of the best guys I know, and this is just the beginning."

Soony Saad fell in front of Toronto defender Gale Agbossoumonde in the second half.

July 13
vs. Toronto FC
at Sporting Park

W 3-0

Sporting Kansas City picked a great time to put together its most comprehensively dominant performance in more than two months. Sporting Park welcomed a record crowd of 21,126 — the 27th consecutive sellout in league play — to watch coach Peter Vermes' crew rough up Toronto FC and move into first place in the Eastern Conference.

"We set the bar now and we know what we're able to do," said goalkeeper Jimmy Nielsen, who tied Tony Meola's club record with his 49th career victory.

In the 21st minute, third-year striker Soony Saad got his first goal in nearly two years. Given a sliver of space atop the Toronto penalty box, Saad gathered a pass from left back Seth Sinovic, and then delivered a grass-tickling laser inside the left post that goalkeeper Joe Bendik was helpless to stop.

"When he hits the ball, he can overpower a goalkeeper, even though he knows the ball's going there, because he hits it so hard," Vermes said.

And Saad — who last scored in his league debut on his 19th birthday August 17, 2011 — was only getting warmed up. It took all of 29 minutes for Saad to poke home his third career goal off a 50th-minute rebound. Saad scored when Bendik palmed midfielder Graham Zusi's rocket from the right edge of the box right to his feet for an easy putaway and a 2-0 lead.

Toronto FC's frustration boiled over in the 56th minute when midfielder Reggie Lambe was ejected for a reckless tackle from behind against Saad.

"That second goal kind of hurt and then, obviously, the sending off was the

Dominic Dwyer and Toronto defender Steven Caldwell went head-to-head for control of the ball in the second half.

nail in the coffin," said Toronto coach Ryan Nelson. "I always thought, even at 1-0, we would get our chances if we had 11 men. It was probably damage limitation from then on."

Saad set the third goal in motion in the 63rd minute with a through ball to forward Kei Kamara, who centered the ball for midfielder Benny Feilhaber with a one-time touch. Feilhaber unselfishly sent the ball wide to striker Claudio Bieler, who happily tapped his team-leading ninth goal of the season into an empty net.

Nielsen, whose eight shutouts are tied for the league lead, had to make a double save in the 18th minute but saw little additional action and Sporting KC recorded its first shutout since May 12.

Sporting record: 9-5-6

We love ya!

July 20
vs. Real Salt Lake
at Rio Tinto Stadium
Sandy, Utah

W 2-1

During the seventh minute of second-half stoppage time, Sporting Kansas City scratched out a stunning victory.

Defender Ike Opara powered a header past Real Salt Lake goalkeeper Jeff Attinella in the 97th minute off a Graham Zusi corner kick to deliver the full three points for Sporting in a battle of conference leaders. Opara started in place of Matt Besler, who was on international duty. Opara's goal was tied for the latest game-winner in Sporting history.

The turning point came in the 66th minute when Sporting, which trailed 1-0 at the time, gained a man advantage. Real Salt Lake defender Chris Wingert was sent off for a professional foul against Soony Saad. Wingert had set a chippy tone in the first minute when he crushed Sporting forward Kei Kamara with a shoulder to the chin and drew a yellow card.

On the free kick after Wingert's red card, Saad finished off a wild scrum and scored his third goal in the last two games. Kamara kept the ball in Real Salt Lake's box after a poor clearance on the initial service and sent a shot toward goal. Real Salt Lake defender Lovel Palmer whiffed on another clearance, giving Aurelien Collin a chance to poke the ball at goalkeeper Jeff Attinella, who was making his first MLS start. From his back, Attinella tried to swat the ball toward the top of the box, but Sporting forward Claudio Bieler intercepted the ball and nodded it to Saad, who wheeled around and buried a right-footed volley.

Sporting initially went down a goal in the 56th minute. Oriol Rosell's yellow card for taking down Javier Morales set a free kick from 40 yards out, which Morales lofted toward the left post. Goalkeeper Jimmy Nielsen came off his line and leaped to grab the lofted cross, but overran the ball, which trickled off his fingertips to Robbie Findley for an off-balance header and a 1-0 lead.

Real Salt Lake coach Jason Kreis criticized Referee Matt Foerester's performance and the decision to have him officiate the physical, top-of-the-table clash.

"It's his 14th match of his entire career," Kreis said. "He is going to be poor. The referee in a sold-out stadium — it's the wrong game for him to make his 14th MLS game."

Foerester whistled 26 fouls, 15 of them against Sporting KC, and issued seven cautions.

"I thought that we kept our cool really well," coach Peter Vermes said, "and I thought that paid off in the end, because obviously they got their red card and we didn't."

Sporting league record: 10-5-5

The fans speak: Three all-stars from Sporting

Defenders Matt Besler and Aurelien Collin along with midfielder/winger Graham Zusi were chosen on the Fan XI for the MLS All-Star Game against AS Roma at Sporting Park. It is the second All-Star selection for all three Sporting Kansas City players. The Fan XI are not necessarily included on the game-day roster. MLS All-Star coach Peter Vermes will select the roster based on player availability and tactical considerations, but all Fan XI players are All-Stars.

"I might be in his ear a little bit trying to play," Besler said. "I want to be out there."

Vermes gets a longer contract and a vote of confidence

Sporting KC extended Peter Vermes' contract as coach and technical director through 2017.

Vermes took over as the then-Wizards' technical director in November 2006 shortly after OnGoal LLC bought the club and he replaced Curt Onalfo as coach on an interim basis in August 2009. The interim tag was dropped after that season, and Vermes has handled both roles the last four seasons, including back-to-back Eastern Conference regular-season championships and the 2012 Lamar Hunt U.S. Open Cup title.

Vermes didn't initially intend to handle both the technical director and managerial roles, but after the 2009 season that changed.

"At the end of that season, when I had my meeting with the ownership group, I'll never forget when Neal (Patterson) looked at me and said, 'So, are you going to take this thing and fix it?'" Vermes said. "That's basically what he said, and I said, 'Yep, I am.'"

Now, Vermes can't see himself not being so heavily involved in all aspects of the club.

"I love both sides of the business," Vermes said. "The continuous job of trying to find the next player that's going to fit into your team and your organization, the culture of your team — that's fun and exciting.

"The strategy of how to beat your opponent — from the the time you set up your game plan, then training and developing that over the course of the week before taking it to the field and trying execute that — is something I loved as a player and probably will love for the rest of my life."

Vermes also relishes developing players — for example, Graham Zusi, Matt Besler, Roger Espinoza, Soony Saad, Chance Myers. He has been successful doing it.

A player — and a team — underestimated

Seth Sinovic has a dirty little secret: He didn't really want to come play for Sporting Kansas City.

It's odd to think about now, given that Sinovic has played 51 games — all starts — in parts of three seasons since signing with Sporting in May 2011, but the unassuming, steady left back didn't have much interest in joining his hometown team at first.

"My feelings were mixed at the time, because I'd seen where the organization had been the past few years," said Sinovic, who started 18 games with New England as a rookie in 2010 but fell out of favor with manager Steve Nicol and was waived in March 2011.

Sporting KC was about to open its palatial new digs, Sporting Park, but at the time the club was still known league-wide for squeezing its games into the outfield at a minor-league baseball stadium.

Sinovic, 26, a Rockhurst High graduate who played collegiately at Creighton, also didn't see many available minutes with veteran left backs Michael Harrington and Roger Espinoza already on the roster.

"He really wanted to go to Real Salt Lake," Seth's father, Bill Sinovic, confessed in an interview. Sinovic had a trial stint with Real Salt Lake after being waived by the Revs before Sporting coach Peter Vermes called. And now Sinovic has evolved into an integral piece for Sporting Kansas City.

Despite those initial reservations, Sinovic quickly surpassed Harrington on the depth chart and became the starter with Espinoza locking up his own starting spot in the midfield. Sinovic has been entrenched at left back ever since.

Seth Sinovic: "A guy who gives you everything."

"Obviously, I lucked out, and it's been a great situation for me," Sinovic said. "I can't even imagine not wanting to be here now."

In fact, when Sinovic was left unprotected during the 2011 MLS Expansion Draft and selected by the Montreal Impact, he was distraught.

Then came a second blessed call from Vermes. Catching a Montreal-bound Sinovic during a changeover in Chicago, Vermes told him he'd been traded back to Sporting KC.

For its part, Sporting is glad New England and Real Salt Lake gave up on Sinovic.

"He's been underestimated by a lot of people," said Vermes, who said Kansas City planned to draft Sinovic in 2010 but got beaten to the punch by New England.

"He's a quiet dude and more of an introvert, so it takes him a while to get comfortable at a place, but I think he feels good about where he's at with the team right now. I don't know how he'd fit in somewhere else, but for us he fits in the right way."

Sinovic may not turn heads with his play or personality, but what Vermes sees is the consummate pro — a coachable player with an MLS-caliber skill set who gets the job done day after day in training and games.

"He's a plain Jane, a steady Eddie, and that doesn't always catch anybody's eye," Vermes said. "He's fast enough and has all the necessary skills enough, but he's not (Aurelien) Collin — a boisterous guy doing the Collin's Corner who can't help but jump on your radar. But what you get is consistency and a guy who gives you everything he has every time he plays."

Only seven days before, the team celebrated a stunning victory in the 97th minute. But on this night, Sporting Kansas City found how it felt to lose a last-minute match when Montreal netted the game's only goal in the 96th minute.

Montreal Rookie Blake Smith, who entered in the 80th minute, delivered a rolling, left-footed blast from the left side of the box toward the right post. He punctuated his second career MLS goal with a backflip as Montreal's faithful erupted in cheers. The victory brought the Impact within a point of first-place Sporting in the conference standings.

The loss snapped Sporting's three-game winning streak and a six-match unbeaten streak. Montreal ended its five-match winless streak.

Three minutes before netting the game-winner, Smith collected an attempted clearance by Ike Opara and rocketed a dipping, spinning, left-footed drive that goalkeeper Jimmy Nielsen punched over the crossbar to keep the game scoreless.

Nielsen's luck soon ran out.

Off a restart near midfield, Montreal switched the ball to the right side, where Hassoun Camara wound up with the ball in space a few yards inside Sporting KC territory. Camara played a diagonal ball back to the left through a wide-open center of the field, allowing Patrice Bernier to draw the defense with a dummy run to the middle. He let the ball travel on to Marco Di Vaio, who calmly sent the ball farther wide to an unmarked Smith for the game-winner.

"I don't think we had enough numbers behind the ball," coach Peter Vermes said. "We weren't in good starting positions. Unfortunately we leave here with nothing when we should have gotten out of here with at least a point."

Sporting played without star defensive centerbacks Matt Besler and Aurelien Collin. Besler is on the U.S. men's roster for the CONCACAF Gold Cup, and Collin served a one-game suspension for yellow-card accumulation.

Sporting league record: 10-6-6,

July 27
vs. Montreal Impact
at Stade Staputo
Montreal, Quebec, Canada

L 1-0

Back on the field, Feilhaber hopes he has hit his stride

The weight of the world is no longer on Benny Feilhaber's shoulders. Reinserted into Sporting's lineup in early July for the first time since May 19, Feilhaber made an immediate impact, notching his first goal of the season against Chicago.

"When you haven't gotten off the mark yet," Feilhaber said, "that first goal is usually what you need to kind of get going."

Feilhaber was brought in with the idea that he could help unlock opposing defenses and bring a spark to a Sporting KC attack that generated only 42 goals last season. Instead, Feilhaber seemed to fall out of favor as the calendar turned to May.

After starting the first nine matches, Feilhaber made only two starts in the next nine games; in four games he didn't play a single minute.

"It took me a little time to realize," he says, that "maybe I needed a little bit more in the tank."

Early in the season it was said that Feilhaber needed time to adjust to Peter Vermes' high-intensity system, but the adjustment period is over. Now, Feilhaber indicated that the only thing holding him back had been his fitness — and that he was working on it.

"It takes more fitness to be a part of this team than other teams," he says. "I put a lot of pressure on myself, and Peter puts a lot of pressure on his players."

Boiling in the Cauldron

Back in 2001, when Sean Dane and his roommate at the time, Jeff Szajnuk, started going to Kansas City Wizards games, they sat on the lower level at Arrowhead Stadium among a group of 50 or so young, boisterous fans. At the team's next game, Dane and Szajnuk decided to join the club, called the Mystics.

Things have come a long way since. The supporters' group has become the Cauldron, a group whose growing passion has been matched by Dane's own. He's now the leader.

"That's how half the people here got involved," he says. "Some person brings them to a game and says, 'Come with me — you're going to have fun.' Then they have fun and they bring a person.

"Even at an organization that now has 2,000 members and 10,000 followers on Twitter and all of this communication, the heart of it is still that one person bringing another person and conveying the passion that we have found for this team."

The Cauldron actually comprises several smaller supporters' groups that are similarly passionate about Sporting Kansas City. Cauldron members pay $20 to join and buy tickets through the group to sit together on the northeast side of the stadium, where they engage in loud cheers and chants during games.

The Cauldron also organizes events outside of Sporting's games: painting signs proclaiming their support, playing pick-up soccer games and gathering for watch parties. Through membership fees and ticket sales, the Cauldron is largely self-sufficient in creating enough money to cover supplies and tailgate parties.

In turn, Sporting helps the Cauldron by allowing its members to use the stadium's loading docks and hang out in the Members Club after games. The team also provides tickets for away matches to members.

"Not every team in the league has the same communication level with their supporters as we do," says Sporting Park general manager Chris Wyche.

This unique relationship between the Cauldron and Sporting KC's front office has taken years to build. Dane says the real boost came when OnGoal LLC bought the team in 2006. At the time, Dane was a member of the Heart of America Soccer Foundation, which helped in finding and developing OnGoal.

"It took an ownership group and front office staff that understood what the supporters' culture could bring to the stadium and our ability to deliver it," Dane said. "Once we showed them, 'Here is what's possible — just support us in it,' they were on board."

Part of the group's success comes from the wide variety of people involved. Graphic designers have volunteered their time to plan banners. Other Cauldron members have showed up to help paint.

Says Zach Cobb, the Cauldron's director of social media, "Every walk of life is in the Cauldron right now."

Routing the All-Stars: AS Roma forward Junior Tallo was congratulated after scoring in the second half as Sporting's Aurelien Collin, an MLS All-Star, walked past.

July
31
AT&T MLS All-Star Game

at Sporting Park

Everything surrounding the 2013 AT&T MLS All-Star Game, which included several days of revelry before the All-Stars battled AS Roma at Sporting Park, drew rave reviews.

The game, however, turned into a dud. Roma grabbed the lead in the fourth minute en route to a thoroughly lopsided 3-1 victory against the All-Stars.

Roma became only the second international club in MLS All-Star Game history to defeat the "home side," which had been 7-2-1 in All-Star action since adopting the MLS vs. The World format in 2003.

Before a record crowd of 21,175, Roma zapped the energy from the building practically from the opening whistle when Kevin Strootman won a footrace with Sporting KC's All-Star centerback, Aurelien Collin, to a through ball from Alessandro Florenzi. Collin got a toe on the ball with a sliding challenge in the penalty box before Strootman could strike it, but the ball still ricocheted off the Roma central midfielder's shin and inside the right post.

With the MLS All-Stars generating precious few chances, Roma's quick-passing, possession-oriented style continually produced chances.

Still 1-0 at halftime, Roma needed less than two minutes into the second half to pad its lead. Florenzi, who was named the game's MVP, hammered Roma's second goal inside the left post and past Nick Rimando.

The lead grew to 3-0 in the 69th minute when Tallo finished a brilliant passing sequence from Balzaretti to U.S. men's national team star Michael Bradley atop the MLS penalty box.

Roma zapped the energy from the building practically off the opening whistle

Opening night at Sporting's state-of-the-art stadium in Kansas City, Kansas, June 9, 2011.

A city transformed into a soccer hotbed

The massive mural was visible from the office of Robb Heineman, the CEO of Sporting Club, the parent of Sporting Kansas City.

"Welcome to Kansas City," it read, "the soccer capital of America."

The occasion was the runup to the MLS All-Star Game in late July.

"We're kind of using that big mantra this week ... and we really feel that way, whether it's our team, our stadium, the project that we're working on here with U.S. Soccer around the training center that will advance over the course of this fall, whether it's our youth development," he said. "We want to be what soccer really is in America, with the ultimate aim of that to have the U.S. win the World Cup."

The notion of Kansas City as such a cog, as the soccer capital of America, still is audacious and maybe more of a declaration of an aspiration than an arrival.

Sporting Kansas City owners, from left, Greg Maday, Robb Heineman, Neal Patterson, Cliff Illig and Pat Curran.

But any such thought at all would have been preposterous only a few years before.

Only the most ardent fans, a few thousand, attended then-Wizards games, dwarfed in Arrowhead Stadium. They later were relegated to the more intimate but equally inappropriate confines of CommunityAmerica Ballpark.

Attendance grew, but not much beyond a niche audience, and merchandising attempts were futile. At one point, Heineman considered the team "the underperforming unit" of MLS and was embarrassed by it.

All that changed with the radical rebranding and recasting of the franchise in 2011 by Heineman and the rest of the innovative local ownership group that bought the Wizards in 2006 from the Hunt family.

The Cauldron bubbled at the beginning of Sporting Kansas City's first game at its new stadium in 2011. Ryan Frost, right, of Kansas City, made his voice heard.

"The name, 'Sporting,' we knew going into the announcement of the brand that it would be wildly unpopular, right?" Heineman said. "But we also had a vision for where we thought we could get and thought that if we could get to that vision point, 'Sporting' would make complete sense to everybody.

"Because we knew what we wanted to be: What Sporting Club is all about is membership."

The most profound risks, obstacles and rewards have come through the living manifestation of that membership: Sporting Park, the team's gorgeous, intricately planned, futuristic $200 million home that opened in 2011 after a number of exasperating attempts to secure financing had failed.

"You can throw that stadium up against any stadium in the world," Alexi Lalas, who played 30 games for the then-Wizards in 1999, says. "That's a credit to the visionaries — the guys who can look at a desert and see Las Vegas."

It features an array of amenities and gizmos derived from influences all over the tech and soccer worlds.

"Every Tuesday for basically two years from noon to 6, we would sit in a room with the architects (Populous) and design this stadium," Heineman said. "We were involved in, for better or worse, every decision in the building, down to knobs on doors."

All of it is contoured to the consumer "experience," a broad term that Heineman says principal investor Cliff Illig was "just adamant" would drive decisions and that can't be defined in any "one-for-all-thing."

Some 31 different sets of constituents were considered in the process, and if-you-build-it-they-will-come hasn't resonated this much since "Field of Dreams."

The stadium capacity is 18,467, but with standing-room crowds swelling the ranks Sporting averaged more in the 2013 season and has capped season-ticket sales at 14,000.

At the All-Star game in late July, at least, Kansas City was, in fact, the soccer capital of the United States.

— *Vahe Gregorian*

August 3
vs. New York Red Bulls
at Sporting Park
L 3-2

We love ya!

Sporting Kansas City had a chance to grab the Eastern Conference title race by the throat in the last two games, but instead came up with zero points against its chief competition. One week after losing on a 96th-minute goal at Montreal, Sporting's usually stout defense leaked goals in a loss to New York.

It came in front of 21,304 spectators, the largest crowd in Sporting Park history and the club's 28th consecutive MLS sellout.

"Offensively, we came out with a strong attitude and we were flying and flying, but that's the easy part of soccer," goalkeeper Jimmy Nielsen said. "The tough part, and where you have to show you have some (heart), is when you've got to run the other way again. That was not existent today."

Things started well for Sporting, which outshot New York 27-5 and controlled 65 percent of the game's possessions.

In the opening 25 minutes, Sporting

> "The tough part, and where you have to show you have some (heart), is when you've got to run the other way again. That was not existent today."
> — *Jimmy Nielsen*

outshot the Red Bulls 8-1 and seemed to be in control before Red Bulls midfielder Jonny Steele made his third goal of the season in the 27th minute. Still, right before halftime, Sporting pulled even and seemed to grab the momentum.

Forward Soony Saad headed a ball on frame, but Red Bulls goalkeeper Luis Robles made a diving save. With Robles unable to control the ball, the rebound fell to forward Kei Kamara, who jabbed the ball into the net.

But in a six-minute stretch in the second half things fell apart when New York popped in two counterattack goals.

With the match tied, 1-1, Fabian Espindola put the Red Bulls in front in the 63rd minute, though replays showed he might have been offside. Second-half substitute Lloyd Sam, who entered in the 60th minute and assisted on Espindola's tally, delivered the dagger in the 69th minute.

Coach Peter Vermes lamented his team's lack of a killer instinct in the second half.

"We had them on their heels and we didn't go step on them," Vermes said. "That does not make me a happy guy."

Forward Dom Dwyer, who drilled a header off the post in the 82nd minute, notched his first MLS goal in the second minute of stoppage time, heading home a lofted cross from Kamara, but a third goal never came.

Sporting league record: 10-7-6

Left: Kei Kamara consoled Claudio Bieler after Bieler missed a header for goal.
Right: Aurelien Collin and New York's Thierry Henry fought for possession.

August

August 7
vs. Real Esteli FC
CONCACAF Champions League

Estadio Independencia
Esteli, Nicaragua

W 2-0

Playing in its first international competition since 2009, Sporting Kansas City traveled to Nicaragua and started the 2013-14 CONCACAF Champions League with a 2-0 victory.

It was the first of four games in the round-robin group stage in the Champions League for Sporting KC. The team earned a spot in the competition by winning the Lamar Hunt U.S. Open Cup in 2012.

"We were very organized and had great shape in the game," coach Peter Vermes said. "We took our chances well when we got them and, especially in the first half, I thought we were very good in possession.

"The start of the second half, I thought they had a little bit of the game. But then we took it back over and closed the game out really well."

Sporting seized control in the 31st minute when midfielder Benny Feilhaber lofted an out-swinging cross from roughly 30 yards away from Real Esteli's goal toward the left post. Defender Ike Opara jumped over Real Esteli defender Douglas De Souza and sent a rainbow header back across the box and into the upper right corner inches from goalkeeper Justo Lorente's outstretched fingertips for a stunning go-ahead tally.

Dom Dwyer added the insurance goal in the 76th minute for Sporting KC.

The winner of the tournament earns a berth in the 2014 FIFA Club World Cup.

CONCACAF, which features the top club teams from the region, is the Confederation of North, Central American and Caribbean Association Football, the governing body of soccer/football in the region, and one of six continental authorities that administer the sport along with FIFA, the world governing body.

Matt Besler's long road to the top of U.S. soccer

The day before the U.S. men's national team battled Panama last month in a key World Cup qualifier, Sporting Kansas City defender Matt Besler and his family took a stroll to Seattle's Pike Place Market.

"Somebody slides open a window on the second floor of a building as we walk by," Besler's dad, Greg, recalls. "Matt's just in his USA warm-up and the guy hollers down, 'Hey, Matt Besler, good luck tomorrow. Go USA.'"

This is Matt Besler's new life.

The trajectory of his national profile spiked off the charts in recent months as he became a fixture of the U.S. men's remade defense. It's a remarkable rise for the self-described "simple guy" who grew up in Overland Park and graduated from Blue Valley West.

Besler's break came in 2012 after Sporting coach Peter Vermes talked to Jurgen Klinsmann, coach of the U.S. national team, during the MLS All-Star Game, urging him to consider bringing Besler in for a first-hand appraisal. A few weeks later, Klinsmann did just that ahead of a match against Mexico at Azteca Stadium. Besler didn't play, but he was included in the January 2013 camp.

Opportunity presented itself in March when Clarence Goodson was injured. Besler was thrown into the fire for his first meaningful international game and he drew rave reviews.

Besler isn't flashy, but he's smart and steady at a position, centerback, that's defined more by mistakes than successes.

"I saw greatness in him as soon as I came here," goalkeeper Jimmy Nielsen says. "He was one of my favorite from day one. You could see there was a of potential in that guy and he's become awesome centerback. He has a helluva future in front of him."

For Saad, soccer inspiration a father-and-son matter

In the basement of Soony Saad's childhood home in Dearborn, Michigan, there's a library of more than 600 videocassettes filled with matches from the UEFA Champions League, English Premier League and Italy's Serie A.

Saad's rise to national Gatorade high school boys soccer player of the year four years ago — and now to regular starter at forward for Sporting Kansas City — can be traced back to those tapes and the hours Saad spent watching them with his father, Ali, and older brother, Hamoody.

"We used to watch them over and over again and analyze them," Saad says. "That's one thing my dad's very good at. His knowledge of the game is incredible for somebody who's never played it at the highest level."

Ali Saad developed a passion for soccer growing up in Lebanon before he came to the United States in the mid-1980s, settling among eastern Michigan's thriving refugee population. When Ali talks about the game, he speaks about a religious-like passion for soccer and the immense artistry he sees in it.

When Ali had his sons — the boys are the youngest of four Saad children — he encouraged Soony, now 21, and Hamoody, 22, to play soccer. They played in the living room, dueling one-on-one, with the couch or coffee table as the goal. They practiced in the bedroom, using the mattress to cushion landings on bicycle kicks. They waged fierce battles in the yard.

"I was so into soccer and I so badly wanted to instill it in them," Ali says.

"Even now, he's hard on us," Soony says. "At Michigan, when I scored 19 goals, he told me that was the worst soccer he'd ever seen me play." Soony's freshman year he set an all-time Wolverines scoring record and finished second in the country.

Ali doesn't apologize for demanding excellence.

"I was tough in the standard that I demanded and the seriousness of it," Ali says. "I've continued putting pressure on him, because right now he's getting an opportunity that he must deliver on."

Soony, who scored in his MLS debut on his 19th birthday two years ago, made only 13 appearances, including two starts, in his first two seasons with

Soony Saad, heading the ball in front of the net.

Sporting KC. It was humbling experience, but Soony appeared to have turned a corner in the 2013 season.

"I guess looking back now, I know what he was trying to accomplish," Saad says of his father. "I know he didn't want me to settle for just being good.

"I want to be that guy where people say, 'Oh, he's gotten better and better and only continues to get better.'"

August 10
vs. New England Revolution
at Sporting Park

W 3-0

"It's a good place to be," coach Peter Vermes said when Sporting Kansas City moved back into first place in the Eastern Conference.

Forward Kei Kamara provided the first two goals, heading home crosses from the left flank by fellow forward Soony Saad in the 27th and 50th minutes to approving roars from the crowd of 19,988 — the 29th consecutive sellout for an MLS match at Sporting Park. It was the second multigoal game of the season for Kamara, who was making his 14th appearance and 10th consecutive start since returning from a three-month loan to Norwich City of the English Premier League.

"It's so easy," said Saad, who recorded his first multi-assist game starting in place of the injured Graham Zusi. "You just loft it up there and nine out of 10 times, (Kamara's) going to win it."

Statistically, Sporting was dominant from the outset against the defensive-minded Revolution, who entered play with the best goals-against average in MLS, 0.91.

Sporting owned more than 60 percent of the possessions and had 495 total passes compared with 160 for New England.

The breakthrough goal came in the 27th minute, when Saad whipped in a quick cross as left back Seth Sinovic held the defense's attention with an overlapping run. Kamara rose above left back Kevin Alston to meet the left-footed, out-swinging cross 12 yards from goal at the far post, nodding the ball into the left edge for a 1-0 lead.

New England's first shot came in the 30th minute, but Saer Sene's left-footed blast from 25 yards out sailed high and goalkeeper Jimmy Nielsen appeared to have it covered anyway.

The Revolution's best chance to tie the game came 10 minutes later when forward Dimitry Imbongo got behind Sporting KC's back line, but Nielsen smothered the potential equalizer with a sliding chest save.

Five minutes into the second half, Saad delivered a right-footed cross to the near post, Kamara outdueled the considerably shorter Alston and headed the ball into the boal.

From there, New England's comeback fortunes went from bleak to unthinkable. Referee Baldomero Toledo ejected two Revolution players in a game that finished with only 19 players on the field. Imbongo, who got away with a blindside, hockey-style forecheck of Chance Myers away from the ball early in the game and also clocked Matt Besler in the back a few times, was sent off after receiving a second yellow card for elbowing defensive midfielder Oriol Rosell in the throat.

Goal made: Sporting teammates congratulated Kei Kamara, right, on his first-half score.

Goal prevented: Kamara knocked the ball out of the way as New England's Chad Barrett, left, and Stephen McCarthy tried to score in the second half.

Midfielder Andy Dorman joined Imbongo in the locker room after drawing a straight red card for a challenge from behind in the 86th minute against Kamara, who limped off with a sprained ankle. The game finished up with 10 Sporting KC players vs. nine Revolution players.

Eight players who saw minutes three days before against Real Esteli FC in Nicaragua also played in the game against New England, thus enduring a round-trip journey of more than 5,000 miles.

Seth Sinovic, Aurelien Collin, Oriol Rosell, Benny Feilhaber and Soony Saad started both matches, while Peterson Joseph, Lawrence Olum and Dom Dwyer either started or subbed into both matches.

Sporting league record: 11-7-6

We love ya!

August 18
vs. San Jose Earthquakes

Buck Shaw Stadium, Santa Clara, California

L 1-0

During the first half, goalkeeper Jimmy Nielsen made a spectacular diving save on a header by San Jose defender Clarence Goodson. Less than 10 minutes into the second half, it was a different story. The header came from one of the top strikers in the Major League Soccer. The result: Sporting Kansas City dropped a 1-0 decision.

Defender Steven Beitashour sent a cross toward San Jose's Chris Wondolowski at the penalty spot in the 55th minute, volleying a ball that had been deflected. Wondolowski, who is the reigning MLS Most Valuable Player and who set a league record with 27 goals last season, redirected the ball inside the right post and past another fully stretched diving try by Nielsen.

Once again, the decisive goal wasn't without controversy. Sporting saw an offsides penalty that went uncalled.

"I'm tired of it," coach Peter Vermes said. "We lost another point because the refs can't make a call. It's very frustrating. And it's incredibly frustrating to a team when the players are fighting like they are."

Aurelien Collin and Matt Besler never managed to recover and get in front of Alan Gordon, whose run drew both central defenders toward goal, while right back Chance Myers was caught behind Wondolowski, who was credited with his eighth goal of the season.

"Both guys were offsides," Vermes said. "I've seen a still photo and both guys were offsides. It should have been called, but (the assistant referee) was in a bad position."

Before that, the defense had buoyed Sporting, which was forced to play while staring into a setting sun during the first half.

In the 33rd minute, off a Marvin Chavez free kick after Collin picked up his league-leading 10th yellow card, defender Clarence Goodson sent a sizzling header low and on frame. However, Nielsen kept the game scoreless with a spectacular diving save, swatting Goodson's shot to Lawrence Olum for a swift clearance.

The Earthquakes eventually would break through and improved to 4-0-1 all-time against Sporting KC at Buck Shaw.

"The game was very ugly," Vermes said. "Playing games like that is a good lesson for our team if we ever come up against a team like this again; we'll know what to expect."

Forward Teal Bunbury, who subbed on for Claudio Bieler in the 56th minute, troubled San Jose's back line with his speed, while Beitashour appeared to take down Soony Saad as he chased a ball toward the left post midway through the second half with no penalty awarded.

"It was a football tackle, but again the call wasn't made," Vermes said. "It's a travesty when you go into games and this stuff happens time and time again. At some point, it has to be different. It's not right and it's not fair for the amount of work that everybody puts into these games."

Sporting league record: 11-8-6

> **"The game was very ugly. Playing games like that is a good lesson for our team if we ever come up against a team like this again; we'll know what to expect."**
>
> *— Peter Vermes*

August

23
vs. Chicago Fire

at Toyota Park, Bridgeview, Illinois

L 1-0

With four defeats in five games, Sporting Kansas City felt its grip slipping from first place in the Eastern Conference.

"Not every game goes your way, but it's unfortunate ... because we dominated in a lot of respects," coach Peter Vermes said after Sporting lost to the Fire. "We gave up a terrible goal to start the half off and then we're chasing the game all the way through."

It was a familiar story for Sporting KC with a loss on the ledger despite dominating the statistics — 59.3 percent of the possession, an 18-12 edge in shots, more crosses into the box, 17 to 11, and superior passing accuracy, 80 percent to 65 percent.

The Fire broke through in the 13th minute when right back Jalil Anibaba corkscrewed a cross from the right flank to the far post, where midfielder Mike Magee centered the ball with a sliding pass that split right back Chance Myers and centerback Aurelien Collin. Making only his second MLS start, Fire centerback Hunter Jumper dove low and headed the ball in for what proved to be the game's only goal.

"We weren't marked up in the box," Vermes said. "We were sleeping. Defensively, it's terrible on a set piece that started with a throw-in. It was very, very amateur."

Meanwhile, Sporting KC whiffed on several golden opportunities, including two first-half sitters off long throw-ins from Matt Besler.

"We had a lot of quality chances, and we should have put at least one away, but we didn't," Vermes said.

Sporting league record: 11-9-6

27
vs. CD Olimpia

CONCACAF Champions League

Estadio Nacional Tegucigalpa, Honduras

W 2-0

If you're going to travel 3,560 miles and play in a monsoon, you might as well win.

Sporting Kansas City did exactly that in its second game of Champions League play, knocking off CD Olimpia in Honduras, and taking firm control of Group 2.

"It's a humongous result," manager Peter Vermes said. "It's not an easy trip with the travel and everything else. It was an unbelievable tactical performance."

Playing his second match since returning from a strained right quad suffered in the MLS All-Star Game, Graham Zusi chipped a through ball over Olimpia's back line in the 27th minute. Forward Soony Saad collected the pass, beating defender Jose Fonseca in a footrace to the ball then putting Sporting KC in front with a cool, left-footed finish. Benny Feilhaber was credited with a secondary assist on the goal.

Second-half substitute Dom Dwyer, who entered in the 48th minute for Claudio Bieler, made a 70-yard run up the middle of the field. Olimpia's defense appeared to corral Dwyer as he entered the 18-yard box. However, Dwyer turned on Fonseca and was chopped down on a reckless challenge by Carlos Mejia for a penalty in the 67th minute. Saad, who now has five goals across all competitions, whipped the ensuing penalty kick into the left side a minute later.

With the win, Sporting KC, which entered the match tied with Olimpia in the Group 2 standings, moved into first place alone with six points and owned a hefty advantage in goals scored and goal differential.

August 31
vs. Colorado Rapids
at Sporting Park
W 2-1

We love ya!

A deflating draw seemed inevitable. Sporting Kansas City, which had lost four of five games entering a showdown against Colorado on a muggy night at Sporting Park, grabbed a first-half lead, but Edson Buddle's 77th-minute goal put a damper on things.

Desperate to avoid another distasteful result, Sporting bore down in the final 10 minutes and Graham Zusi delivered an 88th-minute game-winner. Most in the crowd of 19,579, the club's 30th consecutive sellout in MLS play, went home happy.

"I can't stress how important that win is for us," said Zusi. "We talked going into this one that it was pretty much a must-win for us. We needed to get back on track and put ourselves in a good spot, which is exactly what we did."

Zusi's fifth goal of the season snapped Colorado's nine-match unbeaten streak and vaulted Sporting into a three-way tie atop the Eastern Conference with the Montreal Impact and New York Red Bulls.

Right back Chance Myers started the game-winning sequence by lofting a cross high into the box from the right flank toward the left post. Forward C.J. Sapong, who had come on in the 79th minute, realized he had no chance to attack the ball and direct a header on frame, so he backpedaled and did the next best thing.

"My first inclination was to drop it off and I could hear him (Zusi) yelling," Sapong said. Zusi collected the pass that Sapong nodded his way and calmly buried a right-footed shot past Rapids goalkeeper Clint Irwin. Ball game.

> "We needed to get back on track and put ourselves in a good spot, which is exactly what we did."
> — *Graham Zusi*

Right after scoring the game's first goal, midfielder Benny Feilhaber received a crush of congratulations.

Colorado Rapids midfielder Dillon Powers missed and Matt Besler succeeded in heading the ball away in first-half action.

"It's no secret that we've been struggling to get some results lately in the league," goalkeeper Jimmy Nielsen said. "The reaction from the guys when Colorado made the equalizer was fantastic."

From the opening whistle, Sporting KC was dominant, controlling more than 70 percent of the possessions in the first 30 minutes. Still, with Colorado packing numbers behind the ball, it had become clear that it would take something special to crack open the Rapids' defense.

Midfielder Benny Feilhaber delivered in that fateful 33rd minute, tucking a wicked 30-yard knuckler high inside left post with the outside of his right foot. Feilhaber's goal snapped a 213-minute scoreless streak, but it wasn't enough by itself. Seven minutes after entering the match in the 70th minute, Buddle unleashed a low roller from 25 yards out toward the right post, which centerback Matt Besler deflected into the other side of the goal.

Aside from the fluky goal, the Rapids' best attacking moments came in the 45th minute, when Sporting survived a four-shot flurry. Rookie Deshorn Brown uncorked a dipping shot early in the first half's final minute, which Nielsen barely tipped over the bar. On the ensuing Dillon Powers corner kick, Colorado got three more point-blank chances, including Hendry Thomas' powerful header into the ground and off the crossbar. Thomas and Gabriel Torres also had rebound chances before centerback Aurelien Collin cleared the threat.

Sporting league record: 12-9-6

Kamara heads for England

Kei Kamara, a favorite among fans of Sporting Kansas City, signed a two-year contract with Middlesbrough FC of the Football League Championship, the second tier of English soccer, after Sporting KC agreed to the transfer.

Kamara, a Sierra Leone national player, concluded his Sporting KC career with 38 goals. He led the team in scoring in each of the last three seasons and had seven goals in 15 appearances, 10 of them starts, this season.

Kamara scored 53 goals in eight MLS seasons with four different teams. He turned 29 on Sunday. Sporting KC was 5-5-2 in 12 matches without him this season.

September

7
vs. Columbus Crew
at Sporting Park

W 3-0

Hello again, first place. And goodbye to a pair of scoring droughts.

Sporting Kansas City strikers Claudio Bieler and C.J. Sapong ended extended dry spells and moved the team back alone atop the Eastern Conference standings. A shorthanded Sporting dismantled Columbus 3-0 in front of a sellout crowd of 19,211.

The win moved Sporting three points ahead of Montreal and New York in the Eastern Conference.

"We just outworked them during the course of the game," coach Peter Vermes said matter-of-factly.

Bieler needed only 7 minutes to do what he had failed to accomplish since July 13 — score a goal. In the second half, Sapong scored for the first time since May 5. In turn, Sporting did what it hadn't done in seven weeks — win back-to-back games in Major League Soccer play.

Saad sandwiched a goal between Bieler's and Sapong's in the 41st minute.

Sporting played without defender Matt Besler and midfielder Graham Zusi, who were away on U.S. men's national-team duty, and without midfielder Peterson Joseph and defender Mechack Jerome, who were with Haiti's national team. Added to that, Sporting KC agreed to transfer Kei Kamara to Middlesbrough FC of the Football Championship League.

"We are motivated any time we have an opportunity to step onto the field, but obviously when you have a lot of guys out, you feel that a little bit more," Sapong said. "Everybody can provide an impact. That's how we approach practice, and that's how we approach games."

Bieler started the scoring. He benefitted from a nifty move from Benny Feilhaber, who drew a penalty kick when the Crew's Will Trapp tripped him in the goalie box. Bieler stepped to the dot and fired the penalty kick low and hard past Columbus goalkeeper Matt Lampson. Saad took his turn next. Vermes has pointed to Saad's emergence as evidence his club would survive without Kamara, Sporting KC's leading goal scorer each of the last three seasons. After collecting a pass from Bieler, he beat his man and

> "We just outworked them during the course of the game."
> — *Peter Vermes*

Soony Saad kicked the ball past Columbus defender Eric Gehrig and scored the second of Sporting's three goals.

buried a shot in the upper right corner from 7 yards away. Lampson stood no chance to slow what turned into Saad's fourth MLS goal of the season in the 41st minute.

"We know we're going to miss Kei and we're going to have some absences from certain key guys," Saad said, "but we're ready to step up."

Sapong, who started for just the second time since June, added the final goal in the 55th minute. Oriol Rosell lofted a pass into the box, and Sapong beat Crew defender Tyson Wahl in the air for a header over the top of Lampson, who left his spot on the line.

Goalie Jimmy Nielsen made one save in posting the shutout.

Sporting league record: 13-9-6

Midfielder Josh Gardner shielded Real Esteli defender Manuel Rosas from the ball in the first half.

September 17
vs. Real Esteli
CONCACAF Champions League

Sporting Park

1-1

For a few minutes, a nightmare scenario loomed as reality. Sporting Kansas City trailed Real Esteli FC, a Nicaraguan club team that had never won an international match in 36 tries. Advancement in the CONCACAF Champions League, which was making its debut at Sporting Park, was in doubt.

Jacob Peterson made sure Sporting KC averted disaster. He came off the bench and scored the equalizer in the 78th minute.

Sporting is atop the Group 2 standings with seven points and a plus-four goal differential.

Real Esteli took the lead in the 54th minute when Rudel Calero headed home a corner kick from Samuel Wilson. Real Esteli came into the match having won seven consecutive titles in Nicaragua's top league. But it was 0-29-7 all-time in international matches dating back to 1991.

It was a stunning goal, primarily because to that point Real Esteli had seemed hesitant to even attempt to generate offense.

Sporting KC had to battle the clock, some serious gamesmanship from Real Esteli, and its hot goal keeper, Justo Lorente. It solved all three in the 78th minute. Graham Zusi played a short corner to Peterson, who beat Lorente by sliding the ball between his legs and into the back of the net. It was a nutmeg, in soccer terminology. Peterson provided some spice at the right instant.

"We were screaming off the bench, because they had everybody at the back post," coach Peter Vermes said. "Jake was standing all by himself, so it was really improvisation. Credit to Graham for seeing it, and it was a great finish by Jake for sure."

Peterson had been on the field for only three minutes before finding a goal when his team needed it most.

21
vs.
Toronto FC

BMO Field, Toronto, Ontario, Canada

W 2-1

"It feels amazing to have a game like this, especially given the type of game it was. We knew it wasn't going to a be a tactical game. It was a battle."

— *C.J. Sapong*

Striker C.J. Sapong has rediscovered his scoring touch. Better late than never.

Sapong notched the first multi-goal game of his career against Toronto, lifting Sporting Kansas City to a sloppy victory. Sporting sidestepped a heavy rain to match a season-best three-game winning streak, pulling the club even with New York atop the Eastern Conference standings.

"In the current situation, this win is ginormous," coach Peter Vermes said. "The conditions, the field, everything was not set up for a pretty game. It was set up for an absolute war."

It wasn't pretty in the least — except for the play of Sapong, who has three goals in the last two MLS matches after scoring just one in the first 28. And a Sapong goal usually spells good news for Sporting KC. The team improved to 16-0-2 when Sapong scores.

"It feels amazing to have a game like this, especially given the type of game it was," Sapong said. "We knew it wasn't going to a be a tactical game. It was a battle."

His teammates made the two goals relatively easy for him. With the soggy field playing unpredictably, Sporting elected to play the ball through the air instead. Twice it proved effective with Sapong.

Sporting opened the scoring in the 18th minute on a beautiful sequence through the air. Graham Zusi started the scoring play from 40 yards out, lofting a crossing pass that found Dom Dwyer. The ball never touched the ground again. Dwyer cushioned a header to an unmarked Sapong, who buried another header past Toronto FC keeper Joseph Bendik. Zusi was credited with a secondary assist, his team-best seventh of the season.

"That's definitely one of those goals you'll watch again and again," Vermes said.

Sapong collected his second goal of the afternoon — and fourth of the MLS season — on another header. He sneaked through a Toronto FC defensive line that fell asleep on a crossing pass from Chance Myers and sent a diving header into the back of the net.

That served as the game-winning goal after Toronto midfielder Darel Russell capitalized late in the first half on a Sporting KC mistake to knot the score. Russell took a pass from Alvaro Rey, who scooped up a careless pass from goalie Jimmy Nielsen to defender Aurelien Collin.

From there, Sporting limped into the halftime locker room, needing Jacob Peterson to clear a potential go-ahead goal off the line to preserve a halftime tie. The club came out with a renewed energy in the second half.

"We took a playbook from the NFL — at the end of the day, it was all about field position (in the second half)," Vermes said. "We needed to get the ball into their end and make them play out of the back. That gave us good field position. The entire second half, we played in their end."

That made for a miserable second half for Toronto FC, which compounded the problem in the 82nd minute when Steven Caldwell was sent off for a red card after a dangerous tackle of Josh Gardner.

Toronto FC manager Ryan Nelsen didn't last much longer. He was ejected in extra time.

Sporting league record: 14-9-6

Aurelien Collin, Jimmy Nielsen and Benny Feilhaber were dejected in goal after Philadelphia made the game's only score.

Sporting KC dominated the first 35 minutes, turning the Philadelphia Union goal into target practice. Nothing got through, but Sporting owned possession time and fired six of the game's first seven shots.

A moment later, Sporting found itself down, 1-0. That's how it finished, and Sporting's three-game winning streak was over.

"At half, it was unbelievable to be down 1-0," goalkeeper Jimmy Nielsen said. "We were completely dominating the game and created chance after chance after chance."

The difference was that Union took full advantage of its one good early opportunity. The goal was no thing of beauty but a team riding a five-game scoreless drought would have accepted even the ugliest of scores. A Union push, its first of the game, resulted in a Michael Farfan short shot that Nielsen stopped with a reflex save. But the ball landed near the foot of Union forward Conor Casey, and he didn't miss the shot past a fallen Nielsen and other Sporting bodies for his 10th goal of the season.

"I couldn't find the ... second ball," Nielsen said. "I couldn't see through my own people. I was hoping for the best that somebody would block the second shot."

When that didn't happen, Philadelphia ended a scoreless streak of 346 minutes.

Scoring chances piled up early and often for Sporting.

"We had way too many chances not to score," coach Peter Vermes said.

"Very frustrating," Dom Dwyer said. "We got unlucky in the first half. We had a few that could have bounced either way."

On this night, they bounced away for Sporting.

Sporting league record: 14-10-6

September
27
vs.
Philadelphia Union
at Sporting Park

L 1-0

Philadelphia goalkeeper Zac MacMath punched away the pass intended for Dom Dwyer.

We love ya!

October

5
vs.
Columbus Crew
at Crew Stadium, Columbus, Ohio

W 1-0

Midfielder Graham Zusi called it a gutty performance, a league-best seventh straight win on the road by Sporting Kansas City.

"It puts us right back into the race for winning the East," Zusi said. "How we finish is now in our hands. We don't have to worry about everyone else."

Sporting ended Columbus' three-match winning streak and crippled its late-season playoff push. Sporting's push, meanwhile, reached full swing.

It hopped on the scoreboard in the 17th minute against Columbus when Zusi lobbed a ball toward the back post, laying up a perfect pass for Ike Opara, who sneaked behind the Columbus defense and headed the ball into an open goal. Zusi notched his team-best eighth assist of the season.

The same combination nearly gave Sporting KC an insurance goal in the second half. Working off a set piece near the corner spot, Zusi lofted a ball into the box, and Opara out-leaped the Columbus defense for another header that reached the back of the net. The referee, however, whistled Opara for a foul, erasing the score.

"You have to be crazy to call that a foul," coach Peter Vermes said. "Here is a great goal-scoring opportunity, he puts it in the back of the net and they take it away."

It would've made the final moments less nerve-wracking.

Columbus played a generous portion of the match in the Sporting KC end, but it failed to turn those into high-quality chances against keeper Jimmy Nielsen, who recorded his 11th shutout of the season.

Sporting league record: 15-10-6

9
vs.
Houston Dynamo
at BBVA Compass Stadium, Houston, Texas

0-0

Sporting Kansas City and Houston played to a scoreless draw and the outcome was all about perspective. Is the glass half-empty? Sure, Sporting missed a shot to clinch a playoff spot outright. Or is the glass half-full? Sporting moved within a point of first-place New York in the Eastern Conference.

As it was, Sporting was thrilled to escape with a point, thanks in large part to goalkeeper Jimmy Nielsen. Houston outshot Sporting 12-4 — 5-1 in shots on goal — and the Dynamo was on the attack early. Nielsen made a pair of dazzling saves in the opening six minutes, one on a point-blank shot by Will Bruin in the goalie box.

"They started off very aggressive and very strong," Nielsen said. "And, well, I just did what I'm getting paid for."

On one of the saves, Nielsen stayed down after twisting his knee, but he remained in the game and said afterward that he was fine.

A draw on the road was gratifying because Sporting was without defender Matt Besler and midfielder Graham Zusi, who were with the U.S. national team. Additionally, Designated Player Claudio Bieler was out with a groin strain and didn't travel with the team.

Sporting league record: 15-10-7

As U.S. soccer established itself, Vermes was there

Peter Vermes is not a braggart. Despite his decorated resume, he doesn't boast much about his career accomplishments. Ask him about scoring in the United States' 2-0 win against Mexico in the 1991 Gold Cup semifinals, though, and Vermes can't help himself.

"I came inside," he recalls, "and I hit a ball with great topspin over the top of the keeper into the far corner, and it really gave us the cushion that we needed. It was a great goal. It really was."

Let's set the stage. A year earlier — in 1990 — the U.S. national soccer team earned a spot in the World Cup for the first time in four decades and Vermes was part of that. But the Americans qualified without having to face Mexico, which had been disqualified by FIFA for using over-age players in a youth tournament. Mexico came into the 1991 Gold Cup, a tournament featuring national teams from around the region, with a 23-2-4 record against the United States. Vermes' goal was the final nail in the coffin in Mexico's first shutout loss to the Americans.

"I think it was the first time we really put a chink in their armor," Vermes says. "That was a turning point for U.S. soccer: We truly dominated teams.

After that, Vermes says, the American team could state confidently: " 'We're not just here to play and show a good performance so we don't get embarrassed.' "

Vermes, now 46 and the coach and technical director of Sporting Kansas City, was part of a groundbreaking group of American players in the late 1980s and 1990s. He was captain of that 1991 U.S. team and also on the 1994 World Cup team. Those are among the many reasons he's being inducted into the National Soccer Hall of Fame.

Vermes was the first American to play in the Hungarian and Dutch first divisions and spent time in Spain. While with Volendam in Holland, Vermes scored five goals in 28 matches.

"When he went over there, he just would not be denied," said Bob Gansler, who was Vermes' coach with the 1990 U.S. team and later with the Kansas City Wizards.

Vermes returned to the U.S. when Major League Soccer started in 1996. After Gansler was hired by the Wizards, he jumped at the chance to acquire Vermes. His addition to the team helped the Wizards win the Supporters Shield and MLS Cup in 2000. Vermes was the league's defender of the year.

"He's driven," Gansler said. "He's absolutely driven. That's his main attribute in life."

He is grateful for those who have made financial commitments to MLS, such as Sporting KC's ownership group. But he also remembers individuals from a quarter-century ago who were essentially volunteers trying to sow the seeds of soccer, whether they were in the U.S. Soccer Federation, the coaches or the players.

Today's soccer players are better for Vermes having set the groundwork.

"You would be surprised, I actually think about that the most," Vermes said. "Having to go overseas and start my profession because there wasn't a viable league, I've seen the progress of the game in this country and I've been a part of it. It's very special to me."

> "He's driven. He's absolutely driven. That's his main attribute in life."
>
> — Bob Gansler

D.C. midfielder/defender Perry Kitchen tripped up Soony Saad and got a yellow card for his effort in the first half. Right: Jimmy Nielsen applauded as Sporting players walked around the field after their victory.

October

18
vs. D.C. United
at Sporting Park

W 1-0

> "That's why I was waiting and waiting and waiting for him. I don't want to give the striker any advice, but there's a different way I want to do it if I was a striker."
> — Jimmy Nielsen

The match wasn't chock-full of the scoring chances that Sporting Kansas City usually generates at home. There wasn't much flow to speak of. It wasn't pretty.

But the victory was precisely what Sporting needed.

Dom Dwyer took advantage of Sporting's best chance of the evening and scored the only goal of the match in the seventh minute. Midfielder Peterson Joseph pressed D.C. United's Perry Kitchen, who hurriedly tried to play the ball back to his goalkeeper.

"(Kitchen) saw me coming halfway through his pass and left a little bit on it," Dwyer said. "I just took it around and finished it off."

D.C. United's Jared Jeffrey had a one-on-one chance and tried to put the ball between goalkeeper Jimmy Nielsen's legs, but Nielsen was up to the challenge.

"Today was a one-against-one, and thank God I closed my legs," Nielsen said. "In that situation, I want him (as close) to me as possible, so I can shut down the angles. That's why I was waiting and waiting and waiting for him. I don't want to give the striker any advice, but there's a different way I want to do it if I was a striker."

Nielsen now has 13 shutouts this season, which leads MLS.

"Two games in a row now," coach Peter Vermes said of the goalkeeper's performance. "That's the kind of save you want your goalkeeper to make for you to keep you in the game."

Defense has become Sporting KC's calling card, and the club is back to its stifling ways. Sporting hasn't given up a goal in three consecutive matches in the most important stretch of the season.

Sporting KC has played better at home this season and walked away with nothing to show for it. Ugly wins trump pretty losses, and Vermes will take as many of the former as he can get.

Sporting KC clinched a postseason berth six days earlier when Philadelphia and D.C. United played to a tie.

Sporting league record: 16-10-7

C.J. Sapong headed the ball over D.C. defender Chris Korb in the second half.

Matt Besler rose over CD Olimpia midfielder Rigoberto Padilla to head the ball in the second half.

October 23
vs. CD Olimpia

CONCACAF Champions League
Sporting Park

0-0

Sporting Kansas City isn't fond of playing to draws, yet on this occasion that was enough. The 0-0 draw against CD Olimpia, the 27-time club champions from Honduras, was the result Sporting needed to advance to the quarterfinals of the CONCACAF Champions League tournament.

Sporting won its three-team group with eight points in four matches.

"For us advancing, being the first time the club was entered into this competition, was a major goal of ours this year," coach Peter Vermes said. "We advanced to the knockout stage and we'll start preparing now for next year."

Sporting came out firing early, in an attempt to put a stranglehold on the match. Olimpia goalkeeper Noel Valladares kept the match even with a flurry of impressive saves.

Teal Bunbury scored in the 35th minute, but he was ruled offside. Sporting thought it had a goal in the 54th minute, but Graham Zusi's goal was waved off by an apparent foul.

Vermes never got an explanation of the call.

The team, which will advance to the quarterfinal series in March 2014, laid its foundation on the road in central America, where it beat both Olimpia and Real Esteli 2-0. Both Champions League matches at Sporting Park were draws.

October 26

vs. Philadelphia Union

at PPL Park, Chester, Pennsylvania

W 2-1

With an extra-time goal from Lawrence Olum, Sporting Kansas City achieved a dramatic 2-1 victory in its regular-season finale. It was Olum's first professional goal since 2010 and countered Philadelphia's game-tying goal four minutes earlier.

"That took unbelievable determination," coach Peter Vermes said of the game-winning goal. "It's all about the opportunity. We talked about that before the game. You don't want to leave these opportunities on the table."

Mission accomplished.

Graham Zusi gave Sporting a 1-0 lead two minutes after halftime when he finished off a chance that started with an in-bounds pass from Matt Besler and subsequent header from Olum. Both players were credited with an assist. After gaining the advantage, Sporting opted to rely on its defense to make the score stand — a defense that entered the day on a three-game shutout streak in MLS play.

It wouldn't be four. Needing a victory to keep its postseason hopes alive, Philadelphia substituted leading scorer Jack McInerney into the game after halftime. He responded. After Sporting negated a rash of chances, McInerney notched the equalizer in the 88th minute. The goal ended Sporting's shutout streak in MLS play at 411 minutes.

"They still had to win the game — a tie did them no good — so we knew we could still create a chance to win the game," Olum said. "We had to hang in there, and we got a good breakaway."

Taking advantage of Philadelphia's aggressiveness, Sporting KC utilized the counterattack. Forward Jacob Peterson nearly regained the lead with a strike from the edge of the box in the 91st minute, but keeper Zac MacMath was ready for the shot.

MacMath didn't have a chance against Sporting's next strike. One minute later, Teal Bunbury found an opening in the goalie box, but he passed up a shot to set up a wide-open Olum, who didn't miss on his point-blank look.

Sporting regular-season final record: 17-10-7

The honors list: Zusi, Besler, Bieler, Collin, Opara

Not surprisingly, midfielder Graham Zusi was selected as Sporting Kansas City's Most Valuable Player. It was the second consecutive season Zusi won the award after sharing MVP honors in 2012 with goalkeeper Jimmy Nielsen.

Zusi, 27, has five goals and 10 assists across all competitions, including eight in MLS play. He also has emerged as a key contributor on the U.S. men's national team, notching three goals and two assists in 18 appearances. Zusi's five game-winning assists tied for the most in MLS this season. He also was selected as Sporting KC's offensive player of the year.

Defender Matt Besler, an Overland Park native, was chosen the club's defender of the year for the third consecutive season. Besler, who also has become a regular alongside Zusi with the U.S. men, is the anchor of a defense that has allowed only 29 goals, the fewest goals in MLS for the second straight season.

Forward Claudio Bieler, the club's first-year Designated Player, was awarded the Golden Boot as the top goal scorer. Bieler has 10 goals. He leads all MLS newcomers and also has four assists this season.

Defender Aurelien Collin was awarded the club's humanitarian of the year award for his service in various capacities in the community. Collin, a two-time MLS All-Star, frequents children's hospitals to visit with kids who are battling life-threatening illnesses.

Ike Opara was chosen as Sporting KC's newcomer of the year.

We love ya!

November

2
vs. New England Revolution

Eastern Conference Semifinals

at Gillette Stadium, Foxboro, Massachusetts

L 2-1

Sporting Kansas City's Aurelien Collin scored at the far post after 67 minutes, giving Sporting a goal that was critical even in a loss. This two-legged series between Sporting and the Revolution will be decided by aggregate goals.

"Our goal gave us a good lifeline," goalkeeper Jimmy Nielsen said. "We're still in it. It's an open game going back to Kansas City. We've got the fans behind us. We'll look forward to that game now."

Sporting might take a moment or two to reflect on the opportunity squandered in the first half, though. The visitors dictated every component of the opening half by imposing their will upon the game and preventing the Revolution from establishing any semblance of rhythm through midfield. The ragged cadence of the early stages allowed Sporting to find its footing and then start searching for ways to expose the Revolution defense.

Most of those avenues appeared when Graham Zusi found himself in space in midfield. Zusi mined for midfield space in the Revolution's 4-1-4-1 setup and slipped into dangerous areas when Sporting obtained possession. His ability to find pockets of space placed the Revolution defense under duress and prompted Lee Nguyen to clear off the line after Chance Myers nearly headed home from the remnants of a corner kick.

"We played with a lot of discipline,"

> **"Our goal gave us a good lifeline. We're still in it. It's an open game going back to Kansas City."**
>
> — *Jimmie Nielsen*

Nielsen said. "We were well-organized. And we were very good on the second balls. We forced the back four to play the long balls up to the strikers. Our center backs won the ball, and our midfielders were good on the second balls. They could play the deep balls to Teal (Bunbury), who was very dangerous and worked very hard for the team."

Bunbury touched a one-time effort just wide of the far post from a Jacob Peterson cross in the early stages, but his best opportunity came 10 minutes before the half. Zusi played him over the top and sent him through in a one-on-one opportunity. The ensuing shot landed in goalie Matt Reis' stomach, handing the Revolution a desperately needed reprieve.

After the break, New England improved enough to pose problems.

Kelyn Rowe conjured up perhaps the Revs' first cohesive move 10 minutes after play resumed when he collected a shoddy clearance and sprayed the ball out to the right flank for Diego Fagundez. He corralled the pass and then placed his feed in a promising position for Juan Agudelo to meet at the near post. Agudelo forced a good save from Nielsen, but the rebound deflected toward the goal line. Andy Dorman found himself in the right spot — one Sporting vehemently argued was offside, but to no avail — and tapped home into the vacated net.

Nguyen later played neatly toward Rowe's run on the right side of the penalty area. Rowe scored in style with a fine, first-time finish to hand the Revs a precious second goal.

Forward C.J. Sapong congratulated Aurelien Collin after Collin's first-half goal while they ran past New England forward Dimitry Imbongo.

Claudio Bieler is alive and well.

Shaking off the rust from a three-week absence, Bieler scored an overtime goal in the 113th minute. The goal gave Sporting a victory in the game and, more important, a 4-3 aggregate-goal victory in the Eastern Conference semifinals over New England.

Coach Peter Vermes said Bieler and he talked recently "and I said to him that there's more soccer to play. (He) didn't understand yet what the playoff environment is like, but the opportunities are going to come. (I told him he) was going to stick one away from us, maybe two."

Sporting will settle for the one. The team now will face Houston in the Eastern Conference finals, another two-game series. It will mark the third straight season the two clubs have met in postseason play.

Bieler was a rather unlikely source of Sporting's prosperity. This was his first playing time in nearly three weeks after falling out of favor in Vermes' lineup.

"He is what he is," Vermes said. "He's a goal-scorer. It's great to see him get his confidence on his goal because we need him down the stretch here."

Sporting got a 79th-minute blast from defender Seth Sinovic, a former

November 6

vs. New England Revolution

Eastern Conference semifinals

at Sporting Park

W 3-1

Aurelien Collin celebrated with defender Seth Sinovic after Sinovic's second-half goal.

In the second overtime, C.J. Sapong headed the ball in front of New England defender Andrew Farrell.

member of the Revolution. Sinovic rifled a shot from the left side to the far post, easily beating New England goalie Matt Reis, to tie the series at 3 total goals each.

Sinovic's second career goal — his other coming in last year's Eastern Conference semifinals — spoiled a potential game-winner nine minutes earlier from Revolution striker Dimitry Imbongo. Imbongo's score, which initially deflated a crowd of 19,031, was the first sign of activity toward goal from New England, which opened in defensive mode after a 2-1 victory in the opening leg of the two-game series in Massachusetts. The Revolution executed that plan for 40 minutes, but not any longer.

The home club controlled 72 percent of the possession in the opening half

Sporting defender Aurelien Collin opened the scoring in the 41st minute — taking advantage of the first mistake of the night from a New England defense forced to play on its heels. It was the shot that finally reached the back of the net, but it was far from the first opportunity.

New England elected to bunker its defense, and even its forwards on its own side of the field, but Sporting was prepared for that style. The home club controlled 72 percent of the possession in the opening half while holding New England without an attempt on goal. Sporting pulled the trigger on 32 shots in the game, with 10 of them on goal.

Above: A fan turned his headdress over to Claudio Bieler, who wore it as he shook hands with Matt Besler after the Sporting victory.

Right: Oriol Rosell got to the ball over Dimitry Imbongo in the second half.

We love ya!

Paulo Nagamura cleared the ball away from New England midfielder Lee Nguyen.

One way to slow down Zeus: New England defender Andrew Farrell pulled on Graham Zusi's jersey.

Right: Seth Sinovic got a celebratory hug from by Oriol Rosell after scoring in the second half.

We love ya!

November

9

vs. Houston Dynamo

Eastern Conference final

at BBVA Compass Stadium
Houston, Texas

0-0

Sporting and Houston kicked off their two-leg Eastern Conference final series without kicking the ball into the net. The scoreless tie meant the second leg would start even under the aggregate-goals rule.

The advantage for the better seed — Sporting is second, Houston fourth — is to play the second game at home.

Houston wasn't exactly crushed by the outcome. The Dynamo, like Sporting, had played extra time three days earlier to qualify for this round. Houston lost midfielder Ricardo Clark to injury midway through the first half and, although the Dynamo had the better scoring opportunities, it appeared neither team had energy near the goal.

"It's a war every time we play Kansas City," Houston defender Bobby Boswell said.

The Dynamo has taken advantage of every postseason chance against its rival. This marks the fourth playoff meeting between the organizations and the Dynamo has won three, including the previous two conference championships. But 2013 has been a good year for Sporting in the season series. The teams played to a pair of draws and Sporting won at Houston in May.

In this game, physical and mental weariness and ragged play were apparent most of the afternoon. There were few high-quality scoring chances.

Sporting survived a dangerous moment early in the second half when Aurelien Collin got enough of Omar Cummings just outside the 18-yard box for a free kick. But Houston couldn't cash in then or a few minutes later when Sporting goalkeeper Jimmy Nielsen easily stopped Cam Weaver's header.

In an especially physical game, Collin may have taken the biggest beating. He wound up on the turf several times, and bumped his noggin a few times.

"I'm OK; I'm good," Collin said. "My nose, the back of my head, the side of my head, I'm used to it."

> **"It's a war every time we play Kansas City."**
>
> *— Bobby Boswell, Houston defender*

The most dynamic opportunity for either team happened 40 minutes into the half after a Besler throw-in at the Sporting goal quickly turned into transition for Houston. Will Bruin got enough space for a rip, and launched a laser toward Nielsen from 35 yards. The ball never seemed to rise above the cross bar until the final moment, over Nielsen's outstretched left glove.

Nielsen, perhaps misreading the force of the shot, smiled, and the 150 or so blue-clad Sporting fans in the corner of the stadium exhaled.

About 10 minutes earlier, Nielsen came up with a terrific save on the best scoring chance of the half with a diving deflection of Oscar Boniek Garcia's curling free kick that seemed destined to sneak in.

Houston put the ball in the net early but the offsides flag was up for Kofi Sarkodie's goal.

"An absolute battle," coach Peter Vermes said. "And we know what the return match will be, a final."

In the first half, Dom Dwyer won this battle for a header over Houston defender Eric Brunner.

November

23

vs. Houston Dynamo

Eastern Conference final

at Sporting Park

W 2-1

Inside a media room resembling the interior of a fish bowl, Dom Dwyer leaned back in his chair, then spent 15 minutes entertaining a pool of reporters with his quick-witted responses.

As the player who made the winning score in the game that sent Sporting Kansas City to the MLS championship, Dwyer was the center of attention. He curved in a goal past Houston goalkeeper Tally Hall in the 63rd minute.

"I've tried to stay calm when I get those chances to score," Dwyer said. "It's something I wanted to improve in my

game. I just stayed patient and finished it off. It was all instinct."

His cool, calm demeanor seemingly came too easily to a player who moments earlier made just the ninth start of his MLS career. It took Sporting's newest regular to finally break down an old nemesis, the Houston Dynamo.

Sporting battled MLS record-low temperatures in the low 20s in disposing of Houston, which had knocked Sporting out of the playoffs in 2011 and 2012.

Sporting finally returned the favor, and it overcame a third-minute goal from Dynamo forward Oscar Boniek Garcia

It took Sporting Kansas City's newest regular to finally break down an old nemesis, the Houston Dynamo.

We love ya!

to do it. C.J. Sapong tied the score in the 14th minute before midfielder Benny Feilhaber chipped a beautiful pass to set up the signature goal of Dwyer's young career.

"He made a good run, I was able to get it where I wanted it, and he did the rest," Feilhaber said. "That goal was a clinical finish."

After two years of playing from behind in the second leg of a two-game series, Sporting KC's defense hunkered down in the back half of the field, which effectively limited the Dynamo's chances at a game-tying goal. Houston got only one shot on goal over the final 30 minutes — a near-post shot from Corey Ashe that goalkeeper Jimmy Nielsen initially bobbled before smothering on the ground.

"We were excited (to play Houston)," Sapong said. "We wanted an opportunity to play them again. We felt like we had unfinished business."

It's finished now. But it looked bleak early.

A pregame program that began with stadium lights off and a loud video introduction fired up a stadium-record crowd of 21,650 at Sporting Park. Only eight minutes later, the crowd was hushed. After a failed Sporting KC clearance, Houston midfielder Brad Davis flicked a pass to Garcia, whose shot deflected off defender Matt Besler and spun into the net.

The lead didn't last. Sporting KC had its best chances of the first half over the ensuing 11 minutes. Chance Myers gave Dwyer a clean look at goal in the eighth minute, but Dwyer's momentum on his run prevented him from making solid contact.

Six minutes later, Sapong turned the next chance into a goal. Houston defender Bobby Boswell inadvertently tapped the ball back toward a wide-open Sapong, who took a quick touch and fired a rope toward the opposite post, freezing Hall. In a season with its shares of highs and lows, Sapong scored his fourth goal since September 7.

"I think a couple of years ago, (if) we go down a goal, we don't react the way we did tonight," midfielder Graham Zusi said. "... When they scored their goal, it didn't feel like it really mattered too much. We knew we had 87 minutes to get back into the game."

And now 90 minutes of play remained to bring Kansas City its first soccer championship in 13 years.

Graham Zusi looked for an opening in front of Houston defender Anthony Arena.

Amidst a storm of confetti, Aurelien Collin and his teammates celebrated their Eastern Conference championship.

Right: Midfielder Paulo Nagamura (6) waved a Sporting KC flag beside the trophy.

Something to shout about: Dom Dwyer, right, embraced C. J. Sapong after Dwyer scored the game-winning goal.

We love ya!

December

7
vs. Real Salt Lake

MLS championship

at Sporting Park

1-1
W (7-6)

About 10 minutes before kickoff, two Major League Soccer officials slowly walked the MLS Cup trophy onto the field and placed it on a podium.

A couple hours later, its fate was known: The trophy was here to stay.

In a league-record 10 rounds of penalty kicks, Sporting Kansas City outlasted Real Salt Lake and prevailed, winning the second MLS Cup in franchise history and the first since 2000. Regulation time ended in a 1-1 draw and two overtimes went scoreless on an afternoon when temperatures hovered in the teens.

Sporting KC won the penalty kicks, 7-6, when Real Salt Lake defender Lovel Palmer banged his shot off the crossbar. That gave the game-winner to Aurelien Collin, who moments earlier buried the first penalty kick attempt of his professional career.

"Nobody wants to see a game like that decided on penalty kicks," Collin said before smiling, "except tonight."

Collin also scored the game-tying goal for Sporting in the 76th minute. He was presented the MLS Cup most valuable player award.

A championship that provided plenty of drama saved its best moments for the penalty kicks.

Real Salt Lake's Sebastian Velasquez shot for the win in the eighth round, but goalie Jimmy Nielsen stoned his attempt. Nielsen made two saves in the 10 rounds. Midfielder Graham Zusi stepped to the dot with a chance to clinch the championship in the fourth round, only to watch his attempt sail high over the bar. The two sides matched makes and misses over four straight rounds before Palmer missed and ended everything.

"Back and forth and back and forth," midfielder Benny Feilhaber said. "Those were some anxious moments just standing there and watching."

Dramatic, intense and full of negated opportunities. The overtime periods had it, too.

Real Salt Lake forward Alvaro Saborio thought he had a go-ahead goal in the 105th minute — which would have marked his second goal of the game — but he was correctly whistled offside on the play. That came after Sporting KC had

A championship that provided plenty of drama saved its best moments for the penalty kicks.

It all came down to this: Jimmy Nielsen, left, fell to the ground after the final penalty-kick miss by Real Salt Lake midfielder Lovel Palmer. Shortly before, Aurelien Collin had made the victorious kick for Sporting Kansas City.

Close encounter: Dom Dwyer tangled with Real Salt Lake defender Chris Schuler trying for the ball.

Wincing all the way: In the second overtime, Matt Besler headed the ball past Real Salt Lake forward Alvaro Saboru.

dominated the first half of overtime. Zusi nearly punctuated that with a goal three minutes into the overtime, but Real Salt Lake keeper Nick Rimando tipped his left-footed shot just over the crossbar.

"There were so many times in the game where (momentum) changed," defender Lawrence Olum said. "It was a perfect storybook ending."

In regular time, Real Salt Lake jumped on the scoreboard first with a beautiful finish from Saborio in the 52nd minute. Saborio used his chest to collect a pass from Kyle Beckerman, then took one dribble and banged a shot into the back of the net.

That put Sporting Kansas City in a familiar position. The club also had trailed in the final legs of the Eastern Conference semifinals against New England and Eastern Conference finals against Houston before battling back to win those series. In a quick team huddle on the field in the second half, defender Matt Besler reminded his team of that.

"We basically just told each other to stay calm," Besler said. "At that point, there (were) still 25 minutes left, which is a lot of time, especially at home. We've proven all year long the last 20 minutes of the game at home really shift in our favor."

They did it again. Off a corner kick from Zusi, Collin put away a header in the 76th minute. That tied the game and breathed life into the crowd of 21,650, which sat through the coldest game in MLS Cup history. It was 20 degrees at kickoff.

"For those fans to sit out there in those conditions was incredible," said coach Peter Vermes, who was a player for the 2000 Kansas City Wizards. "This city and those fans deserved this championship."

They've certainly waited for it.

Sporting KC is Kansas City's first professional sports team to win a championship game at home since the Royals defeated the St. Louis Cardinals in the 1985 World Series.

We love ya!

87

We love ya!

Winning goalie Jimmy Nielsen's MLS Cup runneth over

Nothing has ever been easy for any sports team in Kansas City, which makes 36-year-old Jimmy Nielsen, Sporting's goalkeeper, a perfect fit.

Nielsen came to Kansas City four years ago for a happy ending to a career that included the high of stardom and the low of a gambling scandal that made national headlines back home in Denmark.

In the years since, he is 48-25-27 with 35 shutouts. The Wizards have grown into Sporting, MLS' greatest success story. Last year, the league named him goalie of the year and he helped Sporting to a second straight Eastern Conference regular-season championship.

He has become, perhaps, the team's most recognizable player. The White Puma. You can find meaning in little things sometimes. When the last kick by Salt Lake's Lovel Palmer banged off the crossbar, Nielsen's teammates rushed to him. When the big, shiny trophy came out, Nielsen was the one they gave it to. And when it came time to paint the wall with the championship, it was Nielsen doing the painting.

"This trophy here means a lot to me," he said afterward, before pausing, dropping his head, and closing his eyes. This was Nielsen's second conversation with reporters in the locker room. The first time, he said almost exactly these words, but the pause lasted about 15 minutes. He needed to collect himself. First, he went behind a plastic covering they put up to protect the lockers from the spraying celebration. Then he disappeared to another room.

When he came back, he was reflective. He talked about how far the franchise had come, from playing on a minor-league baseball field to a gorgeous soccer-only facility good enough for World Cup qualifiers. Cars in his new city have Sporting KC stickers now, and they drive by Sporting KC billboards on the side of the roads.

Nielsen was 21

Handwritten and heartfelt, the year 2013 was spray-painted on the wall by Jimmy Nielsen, just below the year of the franchise's last MLS Cup Championship in 2000. Below left: Earlier, Nielsen rushed in to grab a shot in front of Real Salt Lake forward Alvaro Saboru at the end of overtime.

years old when he won the only other championship of his pro career. Then, he was with AaB Fodbold, which won the Danish Superliga trophy. He is 36 now, with a family, and perspective. This means more to him than it might to some others.

For now, he'll enjoy this, every second of it, remembering what it feels like to be a champion again — soaked in champagne and smiles.

— Sam Mellinger

Wearing layer upon layer of insulation and decoration, Sporting fans cheered on through the long, cold match with Real Salt Lake.

MVP Collin: "I kept my calm"

Defender Aurelien Collin was named the 2013 MLS Cup most valuable player, and the honor was well-earned.

Collin scored the game-tying goal in the 76th minute — a header off a corner kick from midfielder Graham Zusi — and then added what proved to be the game-winning penalty kick in the 10th round of kicks.

Not a bad afternoon in a championship setting.

"I was very lucky that Zusi put the ball exactly where I wanted it," Collin said of his goal. "I put my head up and it went through. Thank God that it happened at the money time."

There was a time, Collin said, when he believed he wasn't taking advantage of scoring opportunities, especially off corner kicks. In his three seasons with Sporting, he has solved that problem. There was no better time for it.

In Sporting's 2013 postseason run, Collin scored three goals — more than any other player in Major League Soccer.

"I know I'm a better player now than I was three years ago," Collin said.

However, the day wasn't all positive news for Collin. Real Salt Lake struck first on a play that started with a misguided clearance from him. Kyle Beckerman intercepted Collin's pass, then found Alvaro Saborio, who took one dribble and rifled a shot past goalkeeper Jimmy Nielsen.

Earlier, in the 35th minute, Collin received a yellow card.

Collin: "A better player than I was."

"Salt Lake City has been very smart," Collin said. "Since the first minute, they were trying to get in my head. I didn't respond to their provocations. I was pretty proud of myself because that was pretty strong. I kept my calm and didn't respond to anything. I scored and we won, so I'm pretty happy."

The initial yellow card did little to deter Collin's physical play. In fact, midway through the second half he came close to a second yellow card — which he acknowledged was a possibility. That would have resulted in an ejection.

Instead, he stayed in the game. Sporting needed him.

Collin perfectly placed his penalty kick into the right side of the net, past a diving Nick Rimando. It was the first penalty kick of his professional career, he said, "and hopefully the last."

We love ya!

Democracy of the fans: Sporting's hidden genius

Sporting Kansas City has won the championship trophy, but in some ways the franchise is working on something better, bigger and more important. In some ways, the franchise is working on something the Royals and Chiefs and any professional sports team of any size can and should try to emulate.

To understand, let's go back to Sporting's lowest moment in recent years.

Go back to the middle of January 2013. Sporting KC diehards know what this is about. Casual fans remember. Even people who don't care about the team, soccer, or sports heard about it. This was the official and overdue crumbling of the Lance Armstrong Myth, and with it any last hope that a unique partnership with Armstrong's Livestrong Foundation would avoid disaster for Sporting.

A sports franchise had tied itself to perhaps the most prolific drug cheat in sports history. Repeatedly, and in separate conversations both at the time and recently, Sporting KC executives acknowledged the whole thing was a mistake.

And you should've heard the reaction from the team's fans.

"I wish I could show you," says Robb Heineman, CEO of Sporting Club. "I bet there were 90 positives for every five or 10 negatives."

Sporting KC has built what Heineman calls "a tremendous benefit of the doubt" that borders on sycophancy from its fans and much of the local media. This is a fabulous credit to the organization, achieved through a meticulous brand-building strategy, and

A Sporting KC fan displays her victory banner after Sporting defeated Real Salt Lake.

should be the envy of most every professional team both locally and nationally.

"They're very creative," says Kevin Uhlich, Royals senior vice president for business operations.

"They're very smart about how they've communicated," says Chiefs president Mark Donovan.

Winning is and always will be the most important thing for any sports team. But this is Sporting KC's hidden genius.

People often get it wrong about Sporting Kansas City. It's easy to see why.

You go to a game at Sporting Park with your paperless ticket and connect your phone to the in-stadium wireless and feel the energy in a gorgeous stadium, and it's tempting to think these bells and whistles and technological advances are the parts of the team's success that should be modeled by bigger franchises.

They are not. Part of the reason is sheer scale, and part of it is demographics. Sporting KC can do things that franchises with more fans just can't. It can try things that more established brands just can't.

The Royals and Chiefs have fans who are very much like Sporting's fans, but then they also have more fans who like country music and rap, and who are old enough to remember the Vietnam War.

Sporting's fans skew young, and technologically savvy. The Royals' and Chiefs' fans — and all teams have more information about their customers than ever before — are more like the broader demographics of the country.

So Sporting can be more agile, its messages more direct, and concise. Sporting has done a brilliant job in taking advantage of that. But they've been just as effective with something available to all sports teams, regardless of size.

Adam Yarnevich is a 33-year-old who grew up in Wyandotte County. He is a fan of all three local teams. He regularly goes to games at Kauffman Stadium (he likes the weeknight games most), and when he's not at Arrowhead on a Sunday he's posted up on a couch and in front of a TV. He used to have Chiefs season tickets, and hopes to have Royals season tickets someday. For now, he goes to Sporting games. Part of this is his budget. Part of it is something else.

"The biggest difference," he says, "it's more of a democracy with Sporting and not a dictatorship when it comes to the fan experience. It's not just, 'You will like what we give you.'"

This is Sporting's genius.

They have made their fans part of the group in ways the Royals and Chiefs have slipped in recent years. Some of that is in having more fans, sure. But most of it is that Sporting has set its priorities differently.

Sporting has included fans in their process, everything from asking whether an exhibition game should be at Arrowhead (lower prices) or Sporting Park (more intimate experience) to Rob Heineman tapping kegs in the parking lot. They have a loyalty program that includes Members' Club access, exclusive events and a personal team representative for season ticket holders. When the team made cash-only lines at concession stands, fans were confused, complained, and the next game those lines were gone.

This kind of fan-centric prioritizing plays well in all demographics, young and old, tech-heads and technophobes, Northland and Leawood.

The power of the crowd is enormous, and Sporting's strategy puts that power on their side in key moments where other teams would be fighting it. There is a different kind of loyalty this way, a buy-in that's stronger than a playoff loss or a mistake that finds the club linked to a drug cheat and needing to change the stadium's name.

It's harder to move those bigger ships, so the Chiefs and Royals face challenges Sporting doesn't worry about, but the rewards are more as well. The Chiefs have recently created their own loyalty program, and the Royals are looking into one. Even accounting for more fans, this is the part where the more established brands should learn from Sporting.

This is the hidden genius, and why Sporting's fans feel closer to a franchise they've been made a part of.

— *Sam Mellinger*

We love ya!

2013 Sporting Kansas City Players

#	POS	Player Name	Age	HT	WT	Birthplace
5	D	Matt Besler	26	6'	170	USA
16	F	Claudio Bieler	29	5' 11"	171	Argentina
9	F	Teal Bunbury	23	6' 2"	185	Canada
78	D	Aurelien Collin	27	6' 2"	169	France
11	F	Bobby Convey	30	5'9"	150	USA
25	M	Christian Duke	22	5' 9"	157	USA
14	F	Dom Dwyer	23	5' 9"	180	England
4	D	Kevin Ellis	22	5' 9"	160	USA
10	M	Benny Feilhaber	28	5' 9"	160	Brazil
31	D/M	Josh Gardner	31	5' 10"	167	USA
24	D	Mechack Jerome	23	5' 10"	165	Haiti
19	M	Peterson Joseph	23	5' 8"	132	Haiti
23	F	Kei Kamara	29	6'3"	186	USA
21	GK	Jon Kempin	20	6' 1"	170	USA
18	GK	Eric Kronberg	30	6' 5"	210	USA
12	M	Mikey Lopez	20	5' 8"	160	USA
94	M	Jimmy Medranda	19	5' 5"	150	Colombia
7	D	Chance Myers	26	6'	165	USA
6	M	Paulo Nagamura	30	5' 8"	155	Brazil
1	GK	Jimmy Nielsen	36	6'3"	200	Denmark
13	M	Lawrence Olum	29	6' 2"	185	Kenya
3	D	Ike Opara	24	6' 2"	180	USA
2	D	Erik Palmer-Brown	16	6' 1"	175	USA
37	F	Jacob Peterson	27	5' 10"	165	USA
20	M	Oriol Rosell	21	6'	168	Spain
22	F	Soony Saad	21	5' 10"	165	USA
17	F	C.J. Sapong	24	6' 1"	185	USA
15	D	Seth Sinovic	26	5' 10"	170	USA

2013 Schedule

Date	Opponent	Result	Att.
MARCH			
2	at Philadelphia Union	W 3-1	18,160
9	at Toronto FC	L 2-1	25,991
16	vs Chicago Fire	D 0-0	19,868
23	at New England	D 0-0	12,215
30	vs Montreal Impact	W 2-0	18,609
APRIL			
5	vs D.C. United	W 1-0	18,988
17	at New York	W 1-0	12,338
20	at Los Angeles	L 2-0	25,908
27	vs Portland	L 3-2	20,186
MAY			
5	vs Chivas USA	W 4-0	18,811
8	vs Seattle Sounders FC	L 1-0	18,602
12	at Houston Dynamo	W 1-0	19,004
10	at D.C. United	D 1-1	13,612
26	vs Houston Dynamo	D 1-1	20,876
28	vs Des Moines Menace**	W 2-0	15,621
JUNE			
1	vs Montreal Impact	L 2-1	19,470
12	vs Orlando City SC**	L 1-0	15,981
22	at FC Dallas	D 2-2	16,361
29	vs Columbus Crew	W 3-2	20,128
JULY			
3	vs Vancouver Whitecaps	D 1-1	20,137
7	at Chicago Fire	W 2-1	17,735
13	vs Toronto FC	W 3-0	21,126
20	at Real Salt Lake	W 2-1	19,832
27	at Montreal	L 1-0	20,527

Date	Opponent	Result	Att.
AUGUST			
3	vs New York	L 3-2	21,304
7	at Real Esteli*	W 2-0	N/A
10	vs New England	W 3-0	19,988
18	at San Jose	L 1-0	10,525
23	at Chicago	L 1-0	17,085
27	at Olimpia*	W 2-0	N/A
31	vs Colorado Rapids	W 2-1	19,579
SEPTEMBER			
7	vs Columbus Crew	W 3-0	19,211
17	vs Real Esteli*	T 1-1	18,467
21	at Toronto	W 2-1	12,627
27	vs Philadelphia Union	L 1-0	19,243
OCTOBER			
5	at Columbus	W 1-0	19,107
9	at Houston	T 0-0	16,433
18	vs DC United	W 1-0	18,932
23	vs Olimpia*	T 0-0	18,467
26	at Philadelphia	W 2-1	18,462

** Lamar Hunt U.S. Open Cup
*CONCACAF Champions League

MLS Postseason

Date	Opponent	Result	Att.
NOVEMBER			
2	at New Enlgand	L 2-1	15,164
6	vs New England	W 3-1	19,031
9	at Houston	T 0-0	22,107
23	vs Houston	W 2-1	21,650
DECEMBER			
7	vs Real Salt Lake	1-1	21,650
	(W 7-6 Penalty kicks)		

We love ya!

www.ingramcontent.com/pod-product-compliance
Lightning Source LLC
Chambersburg PA
CBHW042009150426
43195CB00002B/63